Universal City
North Hollywood

Foreword by Guy Weddington McCreary, Historical Consultant

Pictorial Research by Laura Cordova-Molmud

"Partners in Progress" by Robert J. Kelly

Produced in cooperation with
The Universal City—North Hollywood Chamber of Commerce

Windsor Publications, Inc.
Chatsworth, California

Universal City
North Hollywood
— A —
Centennial Portrait

*An
Illustrated
History
by
Tom Link*

Windsor Publications, Inc.—History Book Division
Managing Editor: Karen Story
Design Director: Alexander D'Anca
Photo Director: Susan L. Wells
Executive Editor: Pamela Schroeder

Staff for *Universal City—North Hollywood: A Centennial Portrait*
Manuscript Editors: Michael Nalick, Susan Pahle
Photo Editor: Robin Mastrogeorge Sterling
Editor, Corporate Biographies: Jeffrey Reeves
Production Editor, Corporate Biographies: Justin Scupine
Proofreader: Michael Moore
Customer Service Manager: Phyllis Feldman-Schroeder
Editorial Assistants: Elizabeth Anderson, Dominique Jones, Kim Kievman,
    Michael Nugwynne, Kathy B. Peyser, Theresa J. Solis
Publisher's Representatives, Corporate Biographies: Allison Alan-Lee,
    Gina Waters
Layout Artist, Corporate Biographies: Bonnie Felt
Layout Artist, Editorial: Michael Burg
Designer: Ellen Ifrah

Windsor Publications, Inc.
Elliot Martin, Chairman of the Board
James L. Fish III, Chief Operating Officer
Mac Buhler, Vice President/Sponsor Acquisitions

Library of Congress Cataloging-in-Publication Data
Link, Tom, 1946-
Universal City—North Hollywood : a centennial portrait : an illustrated his-
    tory by / Tom Link ; foreword by Guy Weddington McCreary ; pictorial
    research by Laura Cordova-Molmud.
p. 120 cm. 22 X 28
"Partners in progress by Robert J.Kelly."
"Produced in cooperation with the Universal City—North Hollywood Chamber
    of Commerce, Windsor Publications, Inc., Chatsworth, California."
ISBN: 0-89781-393-6
1. North Hollywood (Los Angeles, Calif.)—History. 2. North Hollywood
    (Los Angeles, Calif.)—Description—Views. 3. North Hollywod (Los An-
    geles, Calif.)—Industries. 4. Los Angeles (Calif.)—History. 5. Los Angeles
    (Calif.)—Description—Views. 6. Los Angeles (Calif.)—Industries.
    I. Cordova-Molmud, Laura. II. Kelly, Robert J. Partners in progress.
    III. Title.

F869.L86N675 1990   90-24996
979.4'94—dc20   CIP

Contents

To my father and mother

Acknowledgments

One of the most unexpected pleasures in the researching and writing of this book was meeting so many local-history enthusiasts, who were remarkably generous with their encouragement, assistance and suggestions.

At the top of the list of those to whom I am especially grateful is Guy Weddington McCreary, who served as the book's historical consultant. Elva Meline, the curator of the San Fernando Valley Historical Society at the Andrés Pico Adobe in Mission Hills was also a great help.

Much of the best material in this book would be missing were it not for their contributions. In addition, their good-natured personal support over many months helped make my research an enjoyable experience.

My thanks to the others who gave me the benefit of their experience, especially editors Pam Schroeder, Michael Nalick, and Susan Pahle; Bruce Cook at the Los Angeles *Daily News;* Craig Howell; "Bus" Blanchard; Mrs. Louise Weddington Carson; Universal Studio's Sherri Seeling; Beverly Garland; Alison Pinsler at the Academy of Motion Picture Arts and Sciences research library; professor James L. Dodson at the Los Angeles Valley College historical museum that is named for him; Bill McCann; Dr. Mark Russick; George Shipley of the Sons of the Golden West; Jerry Belcher of the Los Angeles Community Redevelopment Agency; Walter Laemmle; and Suzanne Dewberry at the National Archives in Laguna Niguel.

This rendering by Carl Oscar Borg, which appeared in the November 1931 issue of Westways *magazine, depicts the historic signing of the Capitulation of Cahuenga in 1847. General Andrés Pico, commander of the Mexican forces, is seated on the right and Lieutenant Colonel John C. Frémont, commander of the American troops, is shown seated at the table on the left. The background of this painting shows the site where today's Universal City now stands. Courtesy, Weddington Family Collection*

Foreword

FACING PAGE: Director Wallace Worsley (left), heroine Patsy Ruth Miller, and star Lon Chaney in full make-up, pose on the set of Universal's Hunchback of Notre Dame in 1923. Courtesy, Marc Wanamaker/ Bison Archives

The vast stretch of land that forms the San Fernando Valley must have provided quite a sight when Senator Charles Maclay gazed down from Cahuenga Pass and declared, "This is the garden of Eden."

In the early days settlers like my great-aunt, who arrived in 1886, and my great-grandfather (Wilson C. Weddington), who laid roots in 1890, flocked to this "garden of Eden" despite the shortage of conveniences. Pioneers had vision, courage, hope, and the senses of personal enterprise and frugality that were needed in order to overcome hardships of the day: droughts, floods, fires, and epidemics.

The area now known as North Hollywood, originally Lankershim, emerged as a small farming community. Fruit orchards were plentiful, and the town soon became known as the "home of the peach." Many children rode their horses to Lankershim Elementary School and left them tied to the hitching post during class, but my mother just walked across the backyard to the school.

But it wasn't all school and work; even nineteenth-century farmers knew the importance of leisure time. Recreation in Lankershim consequently made great strides in 1895 when the Davis family, relations of famous Victorian artist W. Dendy Sadler, arrived here from England. The Davises introduced the sport of tennis to the San Fernando Valley. Many young kids played in the Los Angeles River. Bill McCann and "Bus" Blanchard were members of the Rio Vista River Rats, a rowdy bunch who, in the true spirit of Tom Sawyer, swam in the buff.

There wasn't much time for tennis or skinny-dipping, however. People were busy sandbagging the wash during floods and fighting fires like the one at Hartsook Ranch. The scourge of scarlet fever also took its toll on citizens.

By 1910 the town of Lankershim had streetlights, Ford Model T's, its own Bank of Lankershim, the Businessmen's Association, a commercial core, and the Bonner Fruit Company and Cannery, which employed or otherwise supported most of the community. Tons of fruit were sent east from the Southern Pacific depot, and buckboards transported shipments over the hill to Los Angeles. Adding the trolley car made Los Angeles and Hollywood even more accessible. The trip to Hollywood, which had taken the better part of a day in the 1890s, now only took 20 minutes. Lankershim became the financial, commercial, and farming center of the Valley.

Lankershim had no saloon and little, if any, sin. Even buggy-riding after dark was considered taboo. Instead, people gathered at church or the general store or the post office to chat about the goings-on of the day. The community read the Lankershim *Laconic*, which offered subscriptions for one dollar per year.

In 1914 the Businessmen's Association became the Chamber of Commerce, and civic-minded activists stepped up the push for expansion and recognition of the town, just as they do today. In 1915 that call was answered when Universal City formed what was to become the first community dedicated to moviemaking. At night townspeople could hear the sounds of Curley Stecker's bears and elephants and the other wild animals that were used by the film industry.

Many changes took place in the progressive 1920s: poultry ranching emerged as another major industry; political activity, especially concerning water rights, increased as the significance of Mulholland's aqueduct was realized; and

the City of Los Angeles annexed Lankershim (1923). In 1927 the town was re-named North Hollywood, furthering the community's ties to the motion picture industry.

Kiwanis, Rotary, Women's Club, and other service- and leadership-oriented organizations mustered the community support that led to the establishment of a 96-acre park, a library, and a high school. The Toluca Lake area of North Hollywood developed a shopping village, and Lakeside Country Club opened to cater to the growing colony of movie stars.

Despite the Depression and hard times of the 1930s, which included the great flood of 1938, North Hollywood continued to be one of the fastest-growing areas in the Valley, and the new thoroughfare over Cahuenga Pass opened up major access to the Valley. Local citizens who were around during this era undoubtedly remember the disappearance of our adopted daughter, Amelia Earhart—the famous Golden Girl of Aviation. A seven-foot statue in North Hollywood Park and a regional library that bears her name pay tribute to her memory.

During World War II local men served abroad, and many women—who earned the nickname "Rosie the Riveter"—labored to meet the increased production needs. Tolucans Bob Hope, Dorothy Lamour, and Bing Crosby conducted United States Organizations tours, and the town was nicknamed Bingville for the crooner who sang "I'll Make the San Fernando Valley My Home." I remember that air-raid sirens sounded, blackouts occurred, and rationing decals appeared, but I also remember the positive aspects: 20-cent movies, 30-cent haircuts, and 50-cent double burger/double-thick malt combos. When news of war's end finally came in August 1945, I was at the North Hollywood park pool. People rejoiced, and a huge, wild celebration took place on Lankershim Boulevard.

Although the postwar return of GIs to the Valley created a severe housing shortage, the community of North Hollywood earned a reputation as "a peach of a place to have a home." Bob's Big Boy, Curries Mile High Cone ice-cream shop, drag races, television, bobby socks and poodle skirts became the area's icons during the fifties.

The pace of development quickened in the sixties. MCA acquired Universal Pictures and restarted the famous Universal Studios tours. The 14-story executive office towers and Sheraton Universal hotel were constructed. Freeways opened, and apartments sprang up throughout North Hollywood.

Population of the Universal City—North Hollywood area reached 200,000 in the 1970s. To be sure, this was no longer the little 1890 valley community of 10 ranch families. Citizen

Local North Hollywood beauties flash their best smiles for the photographer in the late 1920s. Courtesy, Universal City—North Hollywood Chamber of Commerce

action committees, coordinating councils, PTA groups, and chambers of commerce united in an attempt to minimize urbanization pains. The fruits of these efforts included a community master plan and formation of the CRA's (Community Redevelopment Agency) 40-acre North Hollywood project, the San Fernando Valley's first such undertaking.

The CRA's Academy Project and the modernization of the Laurel Plaza shopping center, in their beginning stages, were among the significant developments in the 1980s, along with MCA's multibillion-dollar expansion of Universal City, which includes the world's largest motion-picture studio, Texaco's 36-story Universal City Plaza building, the Universal City Hilton and Towers, the Cineplex Odeon 18-screen theater, the CityWalk development, and glamorous restaurants. In 1985 the Universal City—North Hollywood Chamber of Commerce was formed.

Now, as the twenty-first century nears and the area celebrates its centennial, community leaders focus on a new vision. A new police station, library, and superior courthouse are scheduled for construction; two Metrorail stations are on the way; and a billion-dollar investment is anticipated to give North Hollywood's commercial core a tremendous boost. Allowing the rebirth to take place while retaining the area's independence and unique identity is the challenge that lies ahead for North Hollywood, Universal City, and the San Fernando Valley. Rest assured: the Universal City—North Hollywood community is prepared for that challenge, as it always has been.

Guy Weddington McCreary
Historian/Community Leader

Chronology

2000 B.C. Chumash and Shoshone tribes establish villages named Kawengna and Toluca in present-day North Hollywood.

1769 Spanish explorer Gaspar de Portolá enters the Valley

1797 Mission San Fernando Rey de España is founded by Franciscan priests

1810 First water dispute between the Valley and the pueblo of Los Angeles

1819 Golden Age for San Fernando Mission

1821 Mexico gains its independence from Spain

1831 First Battle of Cahuenga Pass

1834 Secularization of San Fernando Mission

1845 Second Battle of Cahuenga Pass; Andrés Pico and Juan Manso lease the ex-mission rancho for nine years

1846 Rancho ex-Mission San Fernando is purchased for $14,000 by Eulogio de Celis (subject to the Pico-Manso lease)

1847 John C. Frémont and Andrés Pico come to terms at Campo de Cahuenga, ending the Mexican-American War in California

1850 California enters the Union as a free state

1854 De Celis sells an undivided half interest in the Valley to Andrés Pico

1869 Andrés conveys his undivided half interest in the Valley to his brother Pío, who in turn sells out to the San Fernando Farm Homestead Association, organized by Isaac Lankershim and Isaac Newton Van Nuys

1871 The Valley is divided north and south, with the southern half going to Lankershim and Van Nuys (with present-day Roscoe Boulevard serving as the dividing line)

1880 Los Angeles Farming and Milling Company formed, and the southern portion of the Valley is one big wheat field

1888 First sale of ready-made fruit ranches by the Lankershim Ranch Land and Water Company

1893 Post office opens in "Toluca," while railroad opens across the street in "Lankershim"

1896 Toluca is renamed Lankershim

1897 Bonner Fruit Company opens processing plant as dusty crossroads town becomes "The Home of the Peach"

1909 Cecil and Chauncy Wilcox begin publication of weekly newspaper called Lankershim *Laconic*

1910 Bank of Lankershim opens and becomes an important financial house for the area

1911 Pacific Electric's Big Red street-cars begin service between Lankershim and Hollywood

1913 Mulholland opens Owens Valley aqueduct

1914 Lankershim Chamber of Commerce founded

1915 Carl Laemmle opens gates of Universal City to the public

1923 Lankershim annexes itself to Los Angeles as the poultry business rivals farming and Lankershim Boulevard becomes the premier thoroughfare in the Valley

1924 Lakeside Country Club opens in Toluca Lake, which soon rivals Beverly Hills in attracting celebrity residents, including Amelia Earhart

1927 Plans for Studio City are announced and Lankershim is renamed North Hollywood; voters approve 100-acre park amid vanishing orchards

1931 North Hollywood Chamber of Commerce becomes Valley-wide headquarters for Depression relief

1938 Flood devastates downtown North Hollywood and leads to construction of flood-control channels

1940 First section of the road now known as the Hollywood Freeway opens on Cahuenga Pass

1942 War-industry buildup intensifies North Hollywood's staggering population growth

1945 Thousands of returning veterans make North Hollywood their home

1955 Valley Plaza and Laurel Plaza shopping centers rival traditional Lankershim Boulevard shops

1959 Music Corporation of America buys Universal City

1960 Ventura Freeway opens through North Hollywood

1964 Universal Studios Tour begins and makes Universal City the fourth most popular tourist attraction in the United States

1979 City of Los Angeles Community Redevelopment Agency approves 740-acre North Hollywood project

1990 Phase One of the 22-acre Academy Project opens, assuring future of Lankershim Boulevard's commercial core; Universal City begins rebuilding back lot after $25-million fire; MCA signs agreement to be bought by Matsushita Electric Industrial Company

The Birthplace of California

Prehistory to 1850

Known in centuries and decades past as Kawengna, Toluca, and Lankershim, the land that is now Universal City and North Hollywood offers a colorful history that is as rich as anywhere west of the Mississippi. Its milestones reflect the most significant trends and events in the history of California and the Southwest.

Because of its prime location at the northern side of Cahuenga Pass, the most important and accessible route over the mountains just north of Los Angeles, Universal City—North Hollywood has become one of the most prosperous and vibrant communities in the United States' most heavily populated county.

The area's first residents were members of the Shoshone and Chumash tribes, who established the village of Kawengna at the base of 1,821-foot-high Mount Cahuenga about 4,000 years ago. An Indian term connoting peace and translated as "hold the arrows because friends are coming," Kawengna was home to several hundred Indians in a valley that was among the most heavily populated areas within 500 miles. A smaller village called Toluca (Shoshone for "fertile valley") was located around the nearby tule marshlands of the Los Angeles River.

Kawengna and Toluca attracted the Indians for many reasons, the most important of which was the area's proximity to the river, which for most of the year was a beautiful, limpid stream whose banks were dotted with willow trees. Today the river is encased in a concrete flood-control channel, but for millennia it was a wildly quixotic stream that frequently changed its course during heavy winter rains. For the Indians' modest needs in the semiarid region, it was considered a remarkably reliable source of water, even during severe droughts. Additionally, the Indians could scale the nearby mountains and hills when a powerful storm rolled in from the ocean and the river threatened to flood.

The hills and the floor of the valley offered a variety of berries, fruits, plants, and animals that were available virtually for the asking. The Indians mashed acorns from the many oaks of the region into a type of flour, which they cooked over hot stones in intricately woven baskets. Quail, deer, antelope, rabbit, and other small animals were also abundant.

The surrounding mountains also provided a natural defense against hostile invaders. The climate was remarkably pleasant, and the Indians' simple mud huts and reed shelters could be quickly rebuilt when, as their folklore interpreted seismic activity, the seven giants that supported the land moved and the earth quaked.

Ignorant of the efficiency of the wheel and the benefits of metal-working, these Indians lived a Stone Age existence, although their lives were usually long and worry-free. Unlike the industrious and bloodthirsty Aztec warriors to the south and the fierce Apaches to the east, the Indians of the valley were content to live off the land and enjoy their sun-kissed environment.

But the Spanish conquistadores to the south had other ideas for them. The

The shining star of early San Fernando Valley history, the Mission San Fernando Rey de España is depicted in this 1883 etching by H.C. Ford. Courtesy, California Historical Society

beginning of the end for the Kawengna and Toluca Indians' centuries-old way of life occurred on Saturday, August 5, 1769. At about midday, Gaspar de Portolá, the new governor of Alta (Upper) California, led over the nearby Sepulveda Pass the first overland expedition traveling from the recently founded mission at San Diego to the fabled bay at Monterey. This Spanish incursion into what later became known as the San Fernando Valley marked the first great milestone in the area's history.

The company's military engineer, Miguel Costansó, described what he saw at the top of the pass as "a large and pleasant valley"; one of the expedition's two priests, Father Juan Crespí wrote in his diary that it was "a pleasant and spacious valley."

On the expedition's return journey the following January, Portolá and his men trekked over the gentler Cahuenga Pass, five miles east of Sepulveda Pass. In a sense, they thus became the first of the area's countless commuters, passing through an area that 200 years later would be called "the gateway to the San Fernando Valley."

In May 1770 Portolá passed through Kawengna for the final time on his second expedition to the north. At Monterey, he boarded a ship and sailed out of history. On the return part of that expedition, the father-president of the Alta California missions, the saintly Father Junípero Serra (who had earlier sailed from San Diego to Monterey), replaced Portolá to scout additional mission sites.

In September 1771 Serra founded Mission San Gabriel Archangel in the valley east of Kawengna, and for the first time the Indians of the village fell under the authority of a foreign power. Soon, the Indians at Kawengna had their own mission. On September 8, 1797, Mission San Fernando Rey de España was consecrated by Father-President Fermín Lasuén, and its name was attached to the valley of the Kawengna Indians.

San Fernando Mission was a day's walk on El Camino Reál (the King's Road) from missions San Buenaventura to the north and San Gabriel to the east and only 19 miles from the tiny pueblo of Los Angeles to

the south. The new mission occupied the home of the pueblo's former alcalde (mayor), Francisco Reyes. Alcalde of Los Angeles from 1793 to 1796, Reyes had been squatting on the land for the past 10 years and had turned over to the padres his primitive adobe hut on the sloping northern edge of the valley.

Named after Ferdinand III, the thirteenth-century Spanish king and saint who had liberated his kingdom from the Moslems, San Fernando Mission began

JO MORA

lawyers in California at that time, and this first controversy between the valley and the city over water rights was quickly settled. The dam was dismantled, but the mission was allowed enough water for it to grow corn, unless the pueblo's supply of water ran short at any time. Remnants of the dam remained visible until the early years of this century.

San Fernando Mission quickly achieved a reputation for prosperity and became a kind of local bank, lending money and goods to nearby ranchos and citizens of Los Angeles. Baptisms and marriages among the Indians increased, and when it was operating at its peak in 1814, San Fernando Mission was home to about a thousand Indians.

While the herds, vineyards, and wheat- and cornfields at San Fernando Mission flourished, the Napoleonic Wars in Europe wrought havoc on the Spanish empire. In 1821 a Spanish army officer in Mexico City declared himself the new emperor of an independent Mexico, and after two years of political infight-

its life with 18 mules, 46 horses, 16 oxen, 310 head of cattle, and 508 sheep that had been donated by other missions. The graceful arches of the Convento building and the towering church (built in 1806 but demolished as a result of the 1971 Sylmar earthquake and then reconstructed in 1974) became local landmarks. Although the intentions of the brown-robed followers of Francis of Assisi were unquestionably beneficent, the strict regimentation and discipline imposed by the friars included whippings and other forms of corporal punishment that were cruelly alien to the gentle Indians.

In 1810 the friars erected a small dam on the Los Angeles River at Kawengna, which created a dispute with the settlers at Los Angeles. The pueblo claimed that under Spanish law it was entitled to an uninterrupted flow of water from the river. There were no

ABOVE: Situated on the sloping northern edge of the San Fernando Valley, the Mission San Fernando Rey de España was consecrated on September 8, 1797. When the mission reached its operating peak around 1814, with some 1,000 Indians in residence, it was a flourishing center of prosperity and activity. Pictured here around 1870, the mission covered most of the land known today as the San Fernando Valley before it was secularized in 1834. Courtesy, California Historical Society

FACING PAGE: Rogeria Rocha was a well-known Fernandino blacksmith and silversmith who at one time owned several acres of land at the Rancho ex-Mission San Fernando. This land was granted to Rocha in 1834, a result of the secularization of the local mission. Pictured in this circa 1890 photograph, Rocha died in 1904 reportedly at the age of 110. Courtesy, Southwest Museum, Los Angeles

RIGHT: The wardrobe of this noble Southern California native woman illustrates the effects the Spanish missionaries had on the early San Fernando Valley residents. Though still steeped in the tradition of her ancestors, she is clothed in western garments and proudly carries a rosary around her wrist. Courtesy, Southwest Museum, Los Angeles

ered that the Indians had no desire to Europeanize themselves and that the mission system was self-perpetuating. One mission at a time, the government stripped the church of its lands.

Mexican rule over California proved to be as chaotic as the Californians had feared it would be. Political upheavals became almost routine in Mexico City, and a dozen Mexican governors ruled California over

ing, a Mexican republic was proclaimed.

Most Californians reacted negatively to the news of Mexican independence from Spain. The mother country had treated Californians benignly, if nonchalantly, and the few pioneers who had settled in pueblos and on ranchos near the missions were skeptical of Mexican control. Some Californians were even beginning to think about independence for California or at least some form of home rule.

For their part, the Franciscan missionaries were openly hostile to the new, anticlerical Mexican government because it intended to "secularize" the missions. This policy involved taking the mission lands from the church and giving them to Indians and army veterans. Although this was Spain's plan from the beginning of its New World colonization, the government and the church had conveniently forgotten it when they discov-

the next 26 years. Some of the men were democratically minded and able public servants; others were tyrannical and flat-out incompetents. Some were Californian; most were Mexican.

Several rebellions were organized against the worst governors, though most Californians offered begrudging tolerance toward the fairer administrators. Twice during Mexico's rule of California, political unrest resulted in military skirmishes in Cahuenga Pass.

In 1831 Manuel Victoria, the most arbitrary and cruelest of the governors imported from Mexico City, banished from Califoria several opponents who demanded democratic reforms. José Carrillo and the American Abel Stearns were the most active, and they were exiled to Baja California. From there, the two led a small army against Victoria, who marched his force south from the capital at Monterey. The two sides met near Cahuenga Pass. In the ensuing fight the governor was severely slashed in the face.

Victoria quickly resigned, and California's previous governor, José María de Echeandía, who had lingered in San Diego after being relieved of his official duties, assumed control of the province from his home. To further cloud the political climate, Captain Agustin Juan Vicente Zamorano almost immediately set up a rival government in Monterey, with the Cahuenga Pass serving as the unofficial border between them.

On February 20, 1845, a second battle, if its military posturing can really be considered a battle, occurred just north of Cahuenga Pass. The newly installed Governor Manuel Micheltorena had inflamed many Californians by bringing with him to the province about 400 brigands who were supposed to bolster law and order. Following Texas' separation from Mexico in 1835, the government to the south sought to discourage any independence movement in California.

But Mexico was losing its grip on California too. Each succeeding year, more American mountain men blazed trails over the Rocky Mountains, more Yankee clippers plied the coast, and more squatters from the United States established homesteads. Making Micheltorena even more unpopular with the citizenry was the fact that he favored returning the missions and their lands to the church and evicting whoever was there.

A cabal of Californians, led by Juan Bautista Alvarado and José Castro, brought 284 men over Cahuenga Pass, where they met Micheltorena's forces. On February 19 and 20, 1845, the Mexicans and Californians exchanged long-range artillery fire on the banks of the Los Angeles River while concerned citizens watched the cannonballs fly from the nearby hills. The reported fatalities were two Californian horses and one Mexican mule, although later reports revealed that the mule recovered from its wounds.

As late as the 1900s, remnants of the artillery duel continued to be unearthed, and today a stone obelisk on a dramatic rise above the end of Nichols Canyon Road marks the spot where local residents watched the battle.

After a truce was called and both sides met in Los Angeles to discuss peace, Micheltorena resigned from office. His successor was the California-born, anticlerical Pío Pico. Thus did the last Mexican governor of California come into office. Shortly thereafter, Pío leased the San Fernando Mission (which had been under state control since its secularization in 1834 and which, in effect, comprised the entire San Fernando Valley) to his brother Andrés and Juan Manso. The term was for nine years at a rent of approximately $1,000 a month.

By 1845 many Californians had despaired over the political instability of the Mexican governors and looked longingly over their shoulders to the United States and the Mexican-American border of Texas. There, the boundary dispute between the two countries was at the flash point, and in Washington President James Polk supported the theory that it was the "Manifest Destiny" of the United States to stretch from ocean to ocean. Many Californians hoped that it was only a matter of time before the Stars and Stripes flew over the Pacific Coast of the United States.

In early 1846 the Mexican government authorized Governor Pico to take whatever steps he deemed necessary to protect Alta California from a foreign takeover. One of Pío's biggest assets was the former San Fernando Mission. On June 17, 1846, Pío effected the first sale of the 120,000-acre San Fernando Valley when Los Angeles resident Eulogio de Celis bought Rancho ex-Mission San Fernando for $14,000, subject to the nine-year lease.

The timing of the purchase was fortunate for the new owner. U.S. forces captured the provincial capital at Monterey three weeks later, an event that the U.S. government regarded as the end of Mexican jurisdiction over California. The Mexican period thus marked the transition of the Valley from church control to private ownership.

For his money, de Celis acquired the Valley, with the exceptions of Rancho Encino, Rancho El Escorpion, and a few hundred acres around the mission. He was the only person ever to hold title to the entire Valley (minus those areas). The purchase price was no doubt inflated by a brief 1842 gold rush in Placerita Canyon, located a few miles north of the mission. For the first time in the fabled history of El Dorado, a small vein of the metal proved that there was gold in California after all.

When war between Mexico and the United States broke out in May 1846, the Americans quickly conquered California. By midsummer 1846, American forces were in control of the entire province. But then an insurrection, led by José María Flores, a captain in the Mexican army, erupted in Los Angeles. Captain Archibald Gillespie and a small American contingent were under siege in Government House, the building that served as U.S. headquarters in Los Angeles. Buttressing the renewed strength of the Mexican force, General Andrés Pico raised a Californian army of uncertain number on the valley side of Cahuenga Pass. His plan was to do battle with about 500 Americans, led by Lieutenant Colonel John Charles Frémont, who were approaching from the north in an attempt to rescue Gillespie.

Frémont, who happened to be leading a scientific and surveying expedition to the West when war broke out and who had been instrumental in creating California's so-called Bear Flag Republic, readied his forces in the hills above the Santa Barbara Mission on a cold and rainy Christmas morning in 1846. By January 6, 1847, units led by Major General Stephen Kearny and the U.S. Navy's Commodore Robert Stockton were on their way to Los Angeles from San Diego.

After fighting two bloody battles with the Californians a few miles south of the Los Angeles pueblo,

on January 11, 1847, Stockton and Kearny proudly marched to the pueblo's main square near Olvera Street with band playing and banners flying. Pico's force remained the only one hostile to the Americans in California.

To fool the Americans about the size of his army, Pico used a classic military trick. Eyewitnesses reported that the Californians came north over the Cahuenga Pass in full view of Frémont and his men camped at the San Fernando Mission. Unknown to the Americans, however, Pico's men next passed unseen through a ravine in what is now Universal City and then came back over the hill. This clever maneuver gave Frémont the impression that Pico commanded a larger number of men than he in fact did.

Frémont wrote in his controversial 1887 memoirs:

We entered the pass of San Bernardo [sic] on the morning of the 12th [January 1847]. In the afternoon, we encamped at the mission of San Fernando, the residence of Don Andrés Pico, who was at present in chief command of the Californian troops. Their encampment was within two miles of the mission, and in the evening, [my envoy] Don Jesus, with a message from me, made a visit to Don Andrés. The next morning, accompanied only by Don Jesus, I rode over to the camp of the Californians, and, in a conference with Don Andrés, the important features of a treaty of capitulation were agreed upon.

A truce was ordered; commissioners on each side [were] appointed; and the same day a capitulation [was] agreed upon. This was approved by myself as military commandant representing the United States, and Don Andrés Pico, commander-in-chief of the Californians. With this treaty of Couenga [sic] hostilities ended, and California [was] left peaceably in our possession; to be finally secured to us by the Treaty of Guadalupe Hidalgo in 1848.

On January 13, 1847, the signing of the Capitulation of Cahuenga took place on the kitchen table of the abandoned six-room adobe formerly occupied by Tomas Feliz and his family at the northern end of Cahuenga Pass. The document was signed by Frémont, Pico, and five officers from both their groups on the veranda under a huge oak tree. Copies of the document, known as the Capitulation of Cahuenga, were signed in Spanish and English.

Frémont gave Pico generous terms, much to the chagrin of Kearny, Frémont's superior officer. Kearny had lost an arm to Pico in the earlier Battle of San Pasqual, fought on his march from San Diego to Los Angeles, and regretted missing this opportunity for retribution at Cahuenga. Among the document's seven points and one supplementary article were stipulations that the laws of the United States would take effect immediately in the area and that all members of Pico's brigade—unseen and unnumbered—would never again bear arms against the United States.

According to the terms of the Treaty of Guadalupe Hidalgo, which about a year later formalized the capitulation at Cahuenga, the United States agreed to pay Mexico $15 million for the area that became California, Arizona, New Mexico, Nevada, Utah, Colorado, and Wyoming and assumed $3.25 million in claims against Mexico. Today, a replica of the historic adobe stands in Campo de Cahuenga State Historic Park at 3919 Lankershim Boulevard, opposite Universal City. Many historians regard it as the birthplace of California and the most historic spot west of the Mississippi. The Spanish language version of the capitulation is now among Pico's papers at the Bancroft Library at the University of California, Berkeley; the National Archives in Washington, D.C., holds the English-language document.

Because the peace agreement was so amicable, Pico at once organized a fiesta for Frémont and his men in a California that was finally at peace. But only a few weeks later, at Kearny's instigation, Frémont was court-martialed for his actions at the time of the capitulation and convicted of insubordination, though President Polk pardoned him. Frémont went on to a distinguished political career and in 1856 became the Republican party's first presidential nominee; but Frémont's strong antislavery position and rumors that he was a Roman Catholic helped to defeat him.

In 1850 California became the 30th state in a nation bitterly divided over slavery and the fifteenth free state, a legacy of its heritage from Mexico, which had outlawed bondage in the 1830s. As California celebrated its new status, the gold rush lured thousands of forty-niners to the state. The San Fernando Valley, which just 81 years earlier had known only Indian villages, was now part of the United States of America.

LEFT: Lieutenant Colonel John C. Frémont signed the Capitulation of Cahuenga on January 13, 1847, on behalf of the American forces. This circa 1850 portrait of Frémont was created from a daguerreotype by the famous Civil War photographer Mathew Brady. Courtesy, California Historical Society

ABOVE: General Andrés Pico played an important role in the early development of the San Fernando Valley. He led his forces against the Americans in California during the war between Mexico and the United States and signed the Capitulation of Cahuenga for the Mexican forces at Campo de Cahuenga on January 13, 1847. Courtesy, Seaver Center for Western History Research, Natural History Museum of Los Angeles County

"This Is the Garden of Eden!"

1851 to 1887

A t first, statehood for California meant little change for the few-score homesteaders of the San Fernando Valley. While "the Conqueror of California," John C. Frémont, was returned to Washington in chains to face court-martial for his actions in Los Angeles, Andrés Pico, the vanquished Mexican general, enjoyed the golden life of a Spanish gentleman.

The tenant of the former San Fernando Mission continued to live in relative splendor under his lease and run the Valley as a vast cattle rancho. More steers grazed in the Valley during the first decade of California statehood than at any other time. Their value had never been greater.

As a tsunami of hungry argonauts reached the gold fields of northern California, for the first time cattle became more valuable for their meat than for their tallow and hide. From 1850 to 1852 California's population jumped from 12,000 to 110,000, and the price of beef quickly rose from $4 to $75 per head. Valley herds numbering several thousand head were driven north, and Southern California became known around the state as "the Cow Counties."

Civilization continued to make inroads into the Valley, however. In 1851 the Los Angeles Court of Sessions, which governed the area until the county board of supervisors was set up the following year, recognized two rights of way through Cahuenga: The first led from Los Angeles to Santa Barbara via the Encino Rancho along what is now Ventura Boulevard. Tulare Road (the approximate route of today's Lankershim Boulevard) went from Los Angeles to Fort Tejon and the gold mines of the north over Cahuenga Pass via the San Fernando Mission.

In 1852 the U.S. Board of Land Commissioners, which Congress had created the previous year to validate Spanish and Mexican land grants in California, held hearings in Los Angeles. Ex-governor Pío Pico was accused of selling the Valley to de Celis at a reduced price because the two were friends. De Celis offered evidence to show that the purchase price for Rancho ex-San Fernando Mission was the highest paid for any of the missions: $14,000.

Pío testified that he had made the sale "under and by virtue of my authority as governor and for the purpose of providing means to carry on the [Mexican-American] war." The board confirmed de Celis' claim three years later and said, "The genuineness of the grant is clearly established, and the circumstances under which it was made so clearly explained, as to leave no doubt but that it was done in good faith."

In 1853 a carreta road opened Cahuenga Pass to oxcart travel. De Celis left Los Angeles for his native Spain and never returned, though he did appoint his friend, artist Edward Vischer, as his representative. The following year, Andrés Pico's nine-year lease on the mission expired, but he decided to stay on and paid $15,000 for an undivided half interest in the Valley.

Despite severe fluctuations in the price of beef throughout the 1850s, Andrés Pico's overall prosperity allowed him to extend the romantic charm of

Before fruit orchards made North Hollywood (then known as Lankershim) famous as the "Home of the Peach," the area was covered with waving fields of wheat and barley. Harvesting scenes like this were commonplace by the early 1880s. Courtesy, Weddington Family Collection

Spanish California's vaqueros, caballeros, rodeos, and fiestas into the American period. He developed a reputation as a warm and generous host and freely offered his hospitality to any and all travelers on El Camino Réal.

At the height of the rancho days during the 1850s, the Valley continued to enjoy a frontier economy. Paper money held little appeal, and most travelers carried neither gold nor silver. The lifestyle of the rancho period reflected the open-door policy of the Franciscan pioneers: room and board in exchange for companionship, news, and stories.

J.E. Pleasants, a member of a party of schoolchildren who stayed with Pico for a week in 1856, described his host's hospitality in lavish terms. Pleasants wrote:

He lived in a luxurious style and had a large household of trained servants, chiefly Indians. His silver and china table service made a brilliant display. His household furnishings were plain but massive and luxurious. The plain old mission furniture was retained, but many an expensive and more ornate piece had been added.

Dinners consisted of five to six courses—all of the far-famed California-Spanish cookery, which no nation, not even the French, has ever excelled. At the midday and evening meals, on the veranda in the evening, we were delightfully entertained by native musicians, who played on three stringed instruments then mostly in vogue—the harp, violin and guitar. They played the dreamy old Spanish airs, which were to me the most enjoyable feature of the day which, with the long rides after stock on a spirited horse, was, in itself, all that the heart of a western boy could desire.

Pico's breeding stables produced the most highly prized mounts in California. Much of the local wealth was spent on saddles, riding costumes, and formal wear. The women wore silk gowns with lace rebozos, while the men's fiesta outfits were adorned with gold fringe. Horses carried elaborate saddles and bridles, some hand-carved or decorated with silver. After mass on Sundays, Pico would organize bull-and-bear fights around the church plaza for his neighbors and friends. Pico counted among his associates the most influential Spanish, Mexican, and American citizens of Los Angeles, then also known as Los Diablos (The Devils).

While the 1850s were mostly bucolic and roman-

tic years for the Valley, the county seat of Los Angeles became a cesspool of desperadoes. At a time when cattle towns from Dodge City to Santa Fe painfully endured the era of the Wild West, Los Angeles—the country's westernmost cattle town—became the wildest of them all. Vigilante committees in San Francisco had chased out scores of lawbreakers, and many of them headed for Los Angeles. Not the least of its advantages was a close proximity to the Mexican border, a handy escape in time of pursuit.

There were homegrown rabble-rousers too. In 1856 Juan Flores and Pancho Daniel organized a small army of banditti with the slogan "Down with the Gringos!" Flores and his men threatened the stability of the local government. With Mexico's revolt from Spain and the United States' conquest of California still recent events, another rebellion was easy to imagine.

A posse led by Andrés Pico tracked the Flores gang through the canyons and hiding places of the hills south of Mount Cahuenga. In February 1857, 11 members of the gang, including its ringleader, were lynched at the top of Fort Hill, near the Los Angeles plaza bordering present-day Olvera Street. Most of the local population witnessed the hangings. As a reward for his efforts in capturing the gang, Pico was made a brigadier general in the California National Guard. As an American citizen, a representative in the state legislature, and a member of the 1852 Presidential Electoral College, Andrés Pico completed his transformation from Mexican renegade to American hero.

A revolution in transportation occurred in October 1858, when the first Butterfield Overland Mail Company stage crossed Cahuenga Pass. The company had been awarded the contract to carry the U.S. mail from St. Louis to San Francisco via Los Angeles and the San Fernando Valley. Two coaches a week passed over the ridge in each direction.

By 1860 the Valley's days as an empire based on the hoof were quickly coming to an end. The gold rush was over. Thousands of cattle had starved to death during the drought of the mid and late 1850s. From Los Angeles, one eyewitness to the decimation of the herds wrote, "Thousands of carcasses strew the plains in all directions a short distance from this city. We believe the stock interest of this county, as well as the adjoining counties, to be played out entirely. Famine has done its work."

Cattle driven in from out-of-state further depressed the price of Valley beef. During the winter of 1862 cattle sold for two dollars per head, the price in

FACING PAGE, BOTTOM: The elaborate trappings of a caballero's attire illustrate the detailed, hand-tooled craftsmanship of the ranchero era. Also utilitarian in style, the ornate leather anquero (saddle) acted as protection for gear carried to the rear of the rider and the trapaderos (stirrups) were often decorated with gold and silver threads. Courtesy, San Fernando Valley Historical Society

BELOW: The hardy vaqueros of Southern California's romantic ranchero period worked long, grueling hours across the vast expanse of the Valley's grazing lands. Courtesy, San Fernando Valley Historical Society

FACING PAGE, TOP: This circa 1860 illustration by artist Edward Vischer depicts daily life at Rancho ex-Mission San Fernando during the glory days of the Southern California rancheros in the mid-1800s. Landowner General Andrés Pico is shown with his adopted daughter Catarina, while visiting the quarters of the former mission's Indians. He was later forced to transfer his property holdings to his brother Pío Pico as the result of extreme financial pressures in 1862. Courtesy, San Fernando Valley Historical Society

1832. Nevertheless, Don Andrés was able to retain his half ownership of the Valley for several more years. On October 8, 1860, a telegraph line was inaugurated through the Valley from San Francisco to Los Angeles. It brought the latest news from San Francisco that had raced for 12 days from St. Louis via Pony Express. In the presidential election of 1860, Abraham Lincoln finished third in Los Angeles County. Secessionist sentiments—pro-confederacy and anti-confederacy—ran high. When news of the outbreak of the Civil War reached Los Angeles on the afternoon of April 24, 1861, many excited citizens thought that an inevitable breakup of the Union would end the 11-year Yankee rule of California.

Rumors were rife that residents of Spanish descent would oppose the Union. Others floated the idea of a Republic of the Pacific, which would stretch from the eastern edge of Texas west to the ocean and from the southern border of Mexico as far north as Vancouver, British Columbia. At the Los Angeles plaza, would-be revolutionaries raised the banner of the Bear Flag Republic as a symbol of their independence.

On May 14, 1861, however, Union troops from Fort Tejon in the Tehachapi Mountains marched through the Valley to reinforce the small garrison at Los Angeles. Any secessionist sentiments were quickly quashed. Several weeks later, the exotic-looking Camel Corps, an experimental unit consisting of 31 dromedaries, caravanned through the Valley. The animals stayed in Los Angeles for several months and then were turned loose to roam the local mountains,

RIGHT: Prepared by the Title Insurance and Trust Company in 1912, this map illustrates the mid-1800s Spanish and Mexican ranchos of the Los Angeles area, including the San Fernando Valley. Courtesy, California Historical Society

FACING PAGE, TOP: Successful stockman and grain grower Isaac Lankershim was so impressed by the agricultural potential of the San Fernando Valley that he established the San Fernando Farm Homestead Association in 1869 in order to acquire Pío Pico's undivided half interest in the Valley. Although a severe drought all but obliterated the association's livestock in 1875, the wheat crop proved to be a prosperous venture. Courtesy, Seaver Center for Western History Research, Natural History Museum of Los Angeles County

FACING PAGE, BOTTOM: A stockholder in the San Fernando Farm Homestead Association, Isaac Newton Van Nuys was instrumental in establishing a successful wheat empire in the southern half of the San Fernando Valley in the 1870s. Courtesy, San Fernando Valley Historical Society

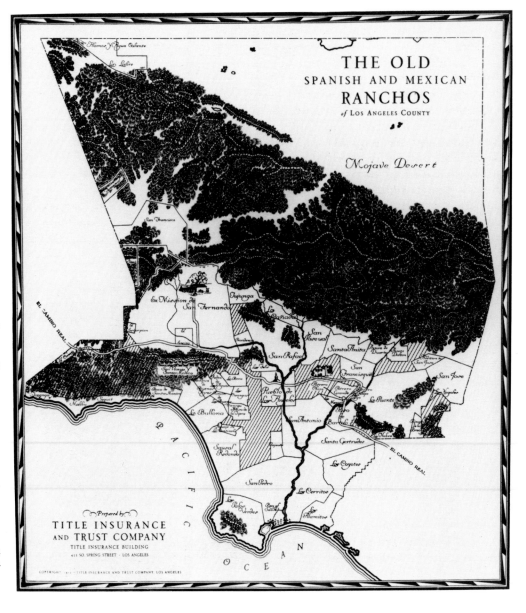

THE OLD
SPANISH AND MEXICAN
RANCHOS
of LOS ANGELES COUNTY

Prepared by
TITLE INSURANCE
AND TRUST COMPANY
TITLE INSURANCE BUILDING
411 SO. SPRING STREET · LOS ANGELES

whose barren nature could not support even the camels.

Don Andrés, like dozens of other Californians, was squeezed economically by the emerging American economy's real-estate taxes, heavy mortgage loans, and high interest rates. Some of the rancheros' mortgages reached 5 percent per month. In May 1862 Andrés could hold out no longer. For $7,000, he transferred his share of Valley property to his brother Pío, who, as the last Mexican governor of California, had originally sold the Rancho ex-Mission San Fernando to de Celis.

In 1863 and 1864 droughts hit hard after several winters of flooding. Once again thousands of cattle died. Like other land-rich, cash-poor owners of the great ranchos, Pío Pico mortgaged his property and went heavily into debt. The New York City speculator who obtained an interest in the Valley from Pico was himself squeezed into making a deal with a Philadelphia financier.

In early 1869 Isaac Lankershim, a native of Nuremberg, Bavaria, who had lived in Northern California for several years and who had acquired huge ranches and farms in Stanislaus, San Joaquin, Fresno, and San Diego counties, rode through the Valley on an inspection trip of his properties. Lankershim, an experienced and successful stockman and grain grower, was impressed by the Valley's high wild oats, which he thought ideal for grazing. Learning of Pío's troubles, he quickly arranged to buy into the area, and the Pico brothers' era of Valley ownership quickly came to an end.

Lankershim joined with several other prominent San Francisco businessmen (including Levi Strauss) to organize the San Fernando Farm Homestead Association. Its purpose was to acquire Pío's undivided half interest for $115,000. (The late de Celis' estate also continued to own the other undivided half interest.)

On March 24, 1871, the Los Angeles District Court split the Valley's 120,000 acres on an east-west axis that paralleled the northern border of Rancho Providencia, which later became Burbank. Lankershim's association gained the southern half, including the land that is now Universal City and North Hollywood. Today's Roscoe Boulevard represents that dividing line.

Two years later, San Fernando Farm Homestead Association stockholder Isaac Newton Van Nuys (who was Lankershim's son-in-law) and Isaac Lankershim's son, James Boon (J.B.), came south to live. J.B. became resident superintendent of the vast ranch. At about this time the association began sheepherding and changed its name to the San Fernando Sheep Company. Van Nuys, however, believed that growing wheat would be more profitable and in 1874 experimented with the crop on several hundred acres that he leased from the association. Van Nuys' first crop of wheat was good enough to justify seeding additional acres.

The following year, drought virtually wiped out the association's herd of 40,000 sheep. But wheat-field production soared. Immediately, grazing was out, farming was in. In 1875 the 3,000-acre wheat crop was heavier than anyone could have reasonably predicted.

While the owners of the southern half of the Valley experimented with sheep and wheat, the northern half became the site of the Valley's first town: San Fernando. In 1873 state senator Charles Maclay, one of the town's founders, rode over Cahuenga Pass on his way to the northern part of the Valley. Looking at the paradise below him, Maclay is reported to have exclaimed,

"This is the Garden of Eden!"

The following year, the town of San Fernando was founded, and the Southern Pacific Railroad connected it with burgeoning Los Angeles. As the nation celebrated the centennial of the Declaration of Independence, Governor Leland Stanford of California presided at a gala golden-spike ceremony inaugurating the $2-million, 6,975-foot-long San Fernando Tunnel, which finally linked Los Angeles with the transcontinental railroad's terminus in San Francisco.

That technological breakthrough made it easier for Lankershim and Van Nuys to ship their increasingly large wheat crops to eastern cities, and in 1880 they formed the Los Angeles Farming and Milling Company. Van Nuys lived and worked on the land, while J.B. Lankershim supervised the company's milling plant in Los Angeles.

In 1884 severe flooding occurred, and Toluca Lake extended one-half mile west of today's Van Nuys Boulevard in Sherman Oaks. Nevertheless, it was said that Lankershim and Van Nuys' wheat crop never failed.

The economic pressure to subdivide the ranch soon proved too powerful to resist. In 1885 the Santa Fe Railroad reached Los Angeles, and a fare war broke out with the Southern Pacific. Cross-country fares dropped lower every week. For a few days, excursion fares from Kansas City hit an all-time low of one dollar. Suddenly, Los Angeles enjoyed one of the biggest booms in the nation's history.

Across the country, thousands pulled up stakes and headed for the land of sunshine and plenty. And to meet the new settlers' needs, a sizable chunk of the Los Angeles Farming and Milling Company was about to be subdivided into picturesque homesteads, the kind of family farm that has come to typify the American Dream.

Sheepherding in the San Fernando Valley was a prosperous enterprise in the 1870s, around the time the San Fernando Farm Homestead Association changed its name to the San Fernando Sheep Company, until the severe drought of 1875 wiped out most of the association's extensive herd. This flock was photographed years later in the 1880s on Weddington ranchland that is now near the intersection of Whitsett and Ventura boulevards. Courtesy, Weddington Family Collection

A One-Horse-Shay Town

1888 to 1914

The Southern California boom of the late 1880s was unprecedented and has never been equaled. From the spring of 1886 to the winter of 1888 as many as 10,000 new settlers arrived in the area each month. Between 1884 and 1890 over 100 new towns were planned for Southern California, though almost two-thirds of them were never built.

In October 1887 J.B. Lankershim and eight other Los Angeles developers (L.T. Garnsey, Dan MacFarland, S.W. Luitwieler, A.P. Hoffman, James R. Boal, F.C. Garbutt, S.B. Hunt, and J.E. Plater) organized the Lankershim Ranch Land and Water Company. Their plan was to purchase for $300,000 about 12,000 acres at the northern side of Cahuenga Pass that belonged to the Los Angeles Farming and Milling Company.

This parcel stretched from 1,350 feet north of Strathern Street on the north to the crest of the Santa Monica Mountains on the south and from the new town of Burbank on the east to Encino Avenue (now Whitsett Avenue) on the west. The property included the land that is now Universal City and North Hollywood and most of Studio City and Sun Valley (then known as the community of Roscoe, from which Roscoe Boulevard derived its name).

Since 1882 those 12,000 acres had been run by J.B. Lankershim and had come to be called the Lankershim Ranch. W.H. Andrews, who had worked for Lankershim on his ranch and who had been in charge of transforming Rancho Providencia into Burbank in 1887, was made superintendent and resident manager in charge of sales for the area's first subdivision.

Andrews, who had moved from Iowa in 1886 with his wife, the former Mollie Weddington, lived in the tract's only building, a ranch house on what is now Vineland Avenue, just south of Third Street (today's Riverside Drive). A crew of 120 Chinese workmen and 200 mules cleared the land of trees, brush, cactus, and stubble. A few cannonballs from the 1845 Battle of Cahuenga were unearthed. Streets were planned a half-mile apart.

Unlike other Southern California developments whose chief crop was the orange, the Lankershim Ranch subdivision focused on a cornucopia of deciduous fruits and nuts, especially peaches, apples, pears, apricots, and walnuts. The area's sandy loam soil was rich in iron and retained moisture to a remarkable degree. An abundant underground water table that was only a few feet from the surface insured the practicality of dry farming. Irrigation was out of the question anyway because the water in the Los Angeles River technically belonged to the city of Los Angeles.

The company planned to sell ready-made ranches, and Andrews and his men soon began the planting of 50,000 fruit and nut trees. At some locations, the first trees failed, and several replantings were necessary. On April 1, 1888, newspaper ads, flyers, and broadsides announced to the public the sale of Lankershim Ranch Land and Water Company lots.

Advertising the land at $120 per acre, the company subdivided its hold-

Lankershim's first schoolteacher, Mary Crawford, is pictured here in 1888 with her students on the property of W. H. Andrews. Classes were held in the Andrews' bunkhouse until the permanent schoolhouse opened the following year near Lankershim Boulevard. Courtesy, Weddington Family Collection

ings into parcels of 5, 10, 20, and 40 acres. The dusty road (now Lankershim Boulevard), laid out only a year earlier as a path through the wheat fields, and Central Avenue (now Burbank Boulevard) were graded. A two-story hotel was built at the intersection of what are now Burbank and Lankershim boulevards. A town called Lankershim was envisioned.

In autumn 1888 Mary Crawford taught school to the pioneer families' children in the Andrews' ranch house while awaiting the completion of the new schoolhouse, which the citizens had supported with the town's first bond issue. The next year, the new building welcomed students just west of what became the central business district on Lankershim Boulevard. The school's administration was so progressive that in 1905 it would claim to have the first Edison phonograph in the country to be used solely for educational purposes. Today, Lankershim Elementary School still occupies the site.

During the winter of 1889, General Frémont paid a sentimental visit to the area and identified the ruins of Campo de Cahuenga. Cecil Wilcox opened a general store and was soon joined in the business by his brother, Chauncy. The hotel was renamed the Hotel Cecil in honor of its new owner. Located some 12 miles from downtown Los Angeles, the "town" was little more than a dusty western crossroads.

Then, almost overnight, the great Los Angeles boom went bust. Trains from the east arrived nearly empty. Times were suddenly hard, and some of the town's earliest settlers lost their properties. Real-estate auctions were introduced. At that time only about 10 families lived on the development's 12,000 acres, though the population was slowly growing and would shortly include a list of names that would serve as the founding families of the town: Weddington, Wilcox, Frieburg, Fox, Barnes, Bossuot, Fritz, Morrison, Ijams, Klump, Bakman, Prince, Gregg, Osborne, and Noble.

Wilson C. Weddington's family would become the most influential. In the winter of 1889-90 Weddington came west from Iowa with his wife and sons Guy and Fred, aged 14 and 11, to visit his sister, Mollie, who was married to Andrews. The area stirred Weddington's interest, and soon he bought two parcels at auction.

Apricots and peaches set out to dry at the A.H. Prince drying yard often covered up to six acres. Pictured here circa 1908, the Prince farm was located at the site of today's North Hollywood Park near Magnolia and Tujunga boulevards. Courtesy, Weddington Family Collection

The first parcel was bought for $720 and included 12 acres at what is now the corner of Weddington Street and Lankershim Boulevard; at a second auction, Weddington purchased 20 acres at today's Lankershim Boulevard and Riverside Drive.

The following spring, W.C. and Fred Weddington went back to Iowa for the family's belongings. Returning with them were a cow, calf, crate of chickens, horse and buggy, and most of their house, which was reassembled where the North Hollywood (formerly El Portal) Theater now stands on Lankershim Boulevard.

Cecil Wilcox remembered the area:

[It was] a vast stretch of washes, sage brush, grease wood and cactus, wild and woolly and actually full of fleas. Civilization had not yet touched the spot. Coyotes roamed freely over the plains, flocks of quail whizzed through the air, thousands of rabbits wandered over the landscape devouring everything eatable, and squir-

rels in uncountable numbers cleaned up the crops. Houses and ranches were few and far between. The roads were impassable in many places with dust and sand. Not a convenience in the whole Valley. The closest bath tub was in Los Angeles. Telephones were not even mentioned.

Stove wood was gathered from the floor of the Valley. Kerosene was used in lamps. The medium of exchange was butter and eggs. That was before the day of electricity, automobiles, motion pictures, radios, paved roads. In fact, North Hollywood was just a blank.

Fred Weddington was more succinct. He said, "There were no lights, no gas, no running water, no nothing."

In 1893 President Grover Cleveland appointed W.C. Weddington postmaster of the little community, which was at first named Toluca. The name was suggested by General Charles Forman, who owned the marshlands with that historic Indian name and who grazed his herd of longhorned steers there. Each

day a horse and buggy from Burbank delivered the mail to the Weddington home, which served as the distribution point. The town was practically on the map.

The following year, Guy and Fred Weddington bought the Wilcox brothers' general store, and Weddington senior moved the post office into the back of the family establishment. Business thrived. For the next decade Weddington Brothers' Store was the only enterprise of its kind in the southern half of the Valley.

Despite a brutal mid-decade drought that lasted until the turn of the century, dry farming proved successful. The harvests were big enough to keep most ranchers solvent. In 1894 the Toluca Fruit Growers' Association was organized, and the first telephone line was strung in the Valley.

In 1895 the Southern Pacific Railroad opened a branch line through the Valley. The Chatsworth Limited made one freight stop a day in Toluca, although that name was in conflict with the sign on the new depot, which read "Lankershim." New arrivals still came in via stagecoach. The Davis family moved into the area from England and built a tennis court on their property amid the rabbit warrens, peach trees, and dusty trails.

A trip over the hills to Hollywood and back took the better part of a day, while a trip to downtown Los

FACING PAGE, TOP: Wilson C. Weddington was one of the founders of North Hollywood and was influential in the town's early development. He is pictured here in 1915. Courtesy, Weddington Family Collection

FACING PAGE, BOTTOM: This 1893 view of the Weddington Ranch shows the area which by 1910 became the heart of the town's business district. Courtesy, Weddington Family Collection

ABOVE: The first post office was established in 1893. Then known as the community of Toluca, Wilson C. Weddington was appointed postmaster by President Grover Cleveland. Weddington is seen here sitting on the porch steps of his home, which served as the post office, with his son Fred in the carriage on the left and his son Guy in the carriage on the right. Courtesy, Weddington Family Collection

Angeles and back took three days by surrey. The Cahuenga Pass was a one-lane dirt road that was "paved" with peach and apricot pits. Lankershim and Ventura boulevards were covered with straw. Turkeys ran wild on Cahuenga Pass, and sheep would wander into your house if you left the door open.

Isaac C. Ijams became the justice of the peace, and Fred Weddington was named constable. The controversy and confusion over the town's name continued. With the post office called Toluca and the railroad depot across the street called Lankershim, the local motto became, "Ship the merchandise to Lankershim, but bill it to Toluca."

J.B. Lankershim threatened to exert his considerable influence on the Southern Pacific railroad to cut off service if the town wasn't named in honor of his father. In 1896 the post office was renamed, although the change to Lankershim wasn't officially recognized until 1905.

The fruit business took a huge leap forward in 1897 when J.M. Bonner, a wealthy resident of New Orleans who owned 110 acres of Lankershim ranchland, built a fruit-shipping plant along the railroad tracks just east of the depot. (The sturdy Bonner facility and depot remain at their original sites to this day and are among the oldest structures in the Valley.) Because there was also a large consumer demand for dried fruit, the Prince family erected enormous dryers on their 32-acre ranch along the Tujunga Wash in the area that is now North Hollywood Park.

Summertime brought hundreds of fruit pickers

Tent-lined camps were erected to house the vast influx of summertime workers, who came from Los Angeles and surrounding areas to work in Lankershim's fruit-laden orchards. This early 1900s camp was located on the east side of Lankershim Boulevard, just north of Magnolia Boulevard, in the shade of the eucalyptus trees. Courtesy, Weddington Family Collection

from the city and the surrounding area. Their tent-lined camps became a familiar site under the eucalyptus trees on Magnolia Avenue, while many affluent ranch owners and their families headed for the beach. The town also became a famous source of enormous pumpkins, which the residents proudly referred to as "Lankershim oranges."

In 1896 Mrs. David Kidson began transporting passengers as well as fruit over Cahuenga Pass. For two years she carried travelers in her cart for 25 cents, round-trip. The next passenger carrier was a two-horse, three-seated phaeton, complete with a fringe on the top. A popular resting place was Eight Mile House, a raunchy restaurant, saloon, and gambling parlor located midway through the pass, appropriately eight miles from Los Angeles. Except for the 17 saloons in the comparatively rowdy town of San Fernando, this was the closest that anyone in Lankershim could get to a drink.

By the late 1890s a terrible drought made water precious, as well. Searing temperatures aggravated the situation. The winter of 1898 brought only 4.83 inches of rain, the smallest amount ever recorded for the next half-century. Despite the water shortage, squatters invaded many parts of the Valley, especially the still-undivided area west of Lankershim; however, they were evicted by a forceful combination of court order and hired toughs.

Reviving a feud that went back to the days when the Franciscan priests built a dam on the river at Ka-

wengna, the city of Los Angeles brought suit against all the ranchers of the Valley and claimed not only the right to the surface water but to the subterranean water as well. In 1899 the California Supreme Court decided the case in the city's favor. Valley farmers and residents were prohibited from removing any water from the ground. One observer wrote that the Valley "found its development abruptly cut off and its future condemned."

Real-estate sales plummeted. Few investors or ranchers were willing to buy into an area without water. The residents of Lankershim were forced to quietly draw their water from artesian wells at the Varney and Gregg ranches. Despite the introduction of regular Southern Pacific passenger service on the gleaming Toluca Flyer, the future looked bleak. But the Weddingtons and several other prominent families continued to bet their futures on additional real-estate acquisitions in the town.

Despite the adversity, or perhaps because of it, Lankershim residents banded together in a spirit of small-town camaraderie. Everyday life—what is now called "the quality of life"—was close to idyllic. Small-town neighborliness reached its pinnacle, and practically everyone was on a first-name basis. During emergencies and disasters the townspeople pitched in as one and assisted the victims. When the Varney ranch caught fire, the two-man fire pump was quickly dragged to the scene; still, the acrid smell of charred animal flesh lingered in the air for several days.

On July 29, 1905, the sudden announcement of a proposed city of Los Angeles aqueduct from the Owens Valley astonished Lankershim residents and appeared to provide a totally unexpected solution to their water problem. Local journalists dubbed the aqueduct proposal "the story of the century." Some Los Angeles property doubled in value overnight. The mood in Lankershim was now upbeat.

The proposal needed federal approval, and President Theodore Roosevelt, who felt an affinity for the West and understood its unique water problems, enthusiastically endorsed the project. In June 1907 about 90

FACING PAGE, BOTTOM: The Bank of Lankershim was established in 1910 with Fred Weddington serving as its first president. Henry Myers and C.C. Bowerman, leading community businessmen, were counted among the bank's other officials. Courtesy, Weddington Family Collection

ABOVE: Loaded with canned goods from the Bonner Fruit Company, a Southern Pacific train heads for outlying markets as it rolls past the Diamond Walnuts storage building. Courtesy, Weddington Family Collection

FACING PAGE, TOP: Fred R. Weddington served as Lankershim's constable and president of the Bank of Lankershim in the early 1900s. Courtesy, Weddington Family Collection

percent of the voters in the city of Los Angeles approved the $23-million bond issue, and construction began in September of the same year.

But the aqueduct created a dilemma for Lankershim residents: Los Angeles city officials made it clear that only the city would get the new water. As long as Lankershim and other parts of the Valley remained independent, they would not get any. The resolution to this thorny political dilemma was deferred while construction progressed.

In 1906 local boosters organized a town picnic that culminated in a baseball game, a Lankershim obsession. All businesses closed for the community's once-a-year day. Mass excursions to Venice and hayrides during summer reflected the same all-for-one, one-for-all spirit.

That same year the Hollywood stagecoach was inaugurated with six runs per day in both directions. Though these first buses provided bumpy rides over the newly macadamized pass, they were a marked improvement over the horse and buggy. It was a time of noticeable change. The horseless carriage was making inroads, and progress seemed to be everywhere. As many as six automobiles a day now made the trip over Cahuenga Pass.

In 1907 Guy Weddington bought the Bonner Fruit Company and its fruit orchards for $20,500. Three years later the most modern cannery equipment was installed. Soon, the new cannery became the largest employer in the town. Within a few years, it employed 265 people and shipped as many as 1,200 tons of fruit per season to Philadelphia, Pittsburg, Chicago, St. Louis, and other large Midwestern and Eastern cities where canned peaches and apricots from Lankershim were a refreshing delicacy.

That same year a saloon opened, but only for a brief time. Within 24 hours of its grand opening, a member of the Carrie Nation League burst into the establishment and smashed it with her ax. The God-fearing inhabitants of Lankershim were more likely to go to the town's churches than congregate in a beer hall, especially in 1908, when a deadly epidemic of scarlet fever swept a fear of the eternal through the community.

In January 1909 the Wilcox brothers, Cecil and Chauncy, began the publication of a four-page newspaper, the Lankershim *Laconic*. Local wags called the paper a "try-weekly": the publishers "tried" to get it out once a week. A year's subscription cost $1.50, and the advertisement-filled newspaper pushed the town into the modern media era.

The *Laconic*'s influence on Lankershim was enormous. Its pages were filled with proud, enterprising boosterism. Powerfully written front-page editorials advocated better roads, a Pacific Electric streetcar line, and flood control.

With the approach of Owens River water, the *Laconic* repeatedly said that prosperity beyond anyone's wildest imaginings was just a few years from the town's grasp. A constant barrage of building-permit statistics gave credence to the almost manic optimism.

By 1910 it was evident that Lankershim—population 850—had indeed survived the worst of its economic doldrums and that it would soon fulfill its early promise. The year brought a quick succession of economic and civic breakthroughs.

Fred Weddington organized the Bank

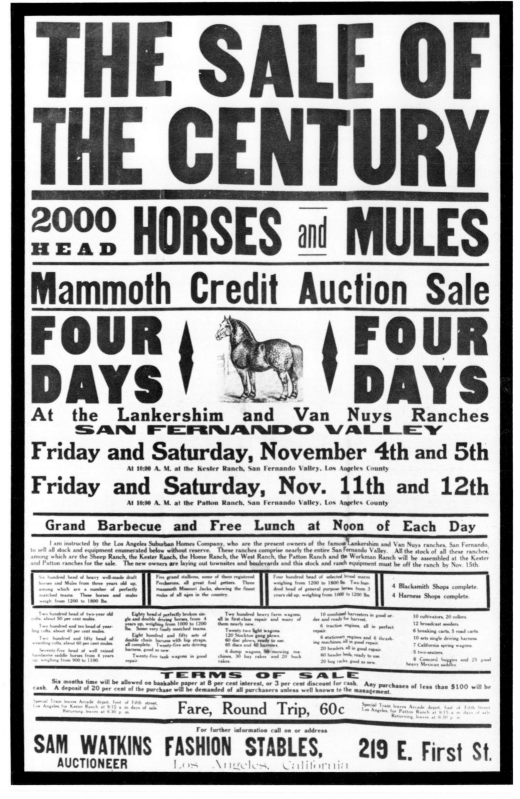

of Lankershim, which opened on Chandler Avenue, near Lankershim Boulevard, on July 25, 1910. Included on its board of directors were such downtown Los Angeles and Valley movers and shakers as H.J. Whitley, Moses H. Sherman, Harry Chandler, William Klump, and Dan Bakman. The composition of the board reflected the bank's importance as a major financial house, and the little town's prestige rose enormously due to its presence and activities. With $75,000 in opening assets, it would claim an impressive 250 depositors by the end of its first year.

With the remainder of the southern half of the Valley being subdivided by the Los Angeles Suburban Homes Company, the "Sale of the Century" was held to sell off the assets of the Los Angeles Farming and Milling Company. Lankershim ranchers attended in droves.

Among the items for sale were 10 combine harvesters, 6 threshing machines, 4 large blacksmith shops, and 2,000 horses and mules. One observer noted, "It was a scene to stagger the imagination. Two thousand stock-

men and farmers entered into active bidding. Six steers were killed daily to provide the free barbecue at noon. The day of the *vaquero* and 24-horse team has passed."

Also in 1910, the Weddington Investment Company was incorporated. In addition, while the Weddingtons sold part of their general store, they constructed an annex in which to expand the remainder of their business. This expansion more than doubled their selling-floor space.

Civic maturity took many forms. Lankershim Boulevard became the first thoroughfare in Southern California beyond the Los Angeles city limits to install electric streetlights. Clare C. Bowerman formed the Lankershim Businessmen's Association (which later became the Lankershim Chamber of Commerce). The road over Cahuenga Pass was improved.

The town moved politically closer to Los Angeles when it joined the city's school district, and the Pacific Electric's Big Red streetcar service over Ca-

Lankershim has a bank, a hotel, a newspaper, two churches, two general merchandise stores, a model grocery, two meat markets, two barber shops, one hardware-and-implement store, one dry-goods store, two blacksmith shops, a livery stable, modern cannery, lumber yard, cement block factory, two fruit dryers. It is the commercial and financial center for the vast improvements going on. The district has a population of about 850. The school is under the jurisdiction of the Los Angeles Board of Education, giving it first rank and allowing Lankershim pupils the privilege of any of the city high schools.

huenga Pass was rumored to be in the planning stage. Tremendous excitement was created by the idea that Lankershim students might soon be able to commute over Cahuenga Pass to Hollywood and attend one of the best high schools in the country.

A Lankershim Development Company advertisement on the back page of the *Laconic* in 1911 dubbed the town "the Home of the Peach," while adding proudly that it had "no saloons" and "no mud." In an editorial the *Laconic's* 1911 First Annual Improvement Edition summed up 20 years of progress:

The resources of the surrounding county are deciduous fruits (which grow to perfection without a particle of irrigation), watermelons, casabas, berries, alfalfa, vegetables, corn and pumpkins. From thirty to fifty wagons go to the Los Angeles market daily in season. The market for all that is grown is right at the door, saving freight charges and commissions. We have the best of advantages in every line to offer.

Guy Weddington's daughter, Louise Weddington Carson, who was born in the original Weddington house in

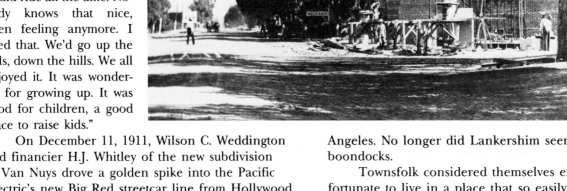

1905 and who now lives a short distance from the site, says, "At that time, Lankershim was a one-horse-shay town. We lived on a farm, and we had more fun than the people in the cities. I was horse-crazy. I would ride all the time. Nobody knows that nice, open feeling anymore. I liked that. We'd go up the hills, down the hills. We all enjoyed it. It was wonderful for growing up. It was good for children, a good place to raise kids."

On December 11, 1911, Wilson C. Weddington and financier H.J. Whitley of the new subdivision of Van Nuys drove a golden spike into the Pacific Electric's new Big Red streetcar line from Hollywood. Lankershim now had regular passenger service to and from one of the fastest-growing metropolises in the country. It was as if the town had been picked up and physically moved closer to Los Angeles. No longer did Lankershim seem out in the boondocks.

Townsfolk considered themselves extremely fortunate to live in a place that so easily combined the best of the city and the country. Hollywood and Lankershim were now separated by a mere 45-minute ride via safe and comfortable streetcars that cost only 25 cents (40 cents for a round trip) and that ran ev-

LEFT: Thousands of spectators gathered to watch the opening of the Owens Valley aqueduct on November 5, 1913. The precious flow of water can be seen cascading down the channel into the Valley below. Courtesy, San Fernando Valley Historical Society

FACING PAGE, TOP: Amid much fanfare and celebration, Wilson C. Weddington and financier H.J. Whitley drove the golden spike into the Pacific Electric's new Big Red streetcar line on December 11, 1911, initiating passenger service from Hollywood to Lankershim. General M.H. Sherman, president of Pacific Electric, was among those present. Courtesy, Weddington Family Collection

FACING PAGE, BOTTOM: Construction to expand and meet the needs of a growing Lankershim was a common sight during the early 1900s. Lankershim Boulevard is seen here before 1915. Courtesy, Weddington Family Collection

ery 15 minutes. On the first day of service, an estimated 500 people took the ride into the city.

Some Lankershim real estate was now selling for $1,000 an acre. Several homes were served by the first electricity lines in the area. Optimism over a resolution to the water problem ran high. The *Laconic* noted the suburbanization and added, "The older residents of Lankershim would complain that the town is growing so fast that they are unable to know who their next-door neighbors are or what they are doing."

Most important of all, the great transforming event in the history of Southern California occurred on Wednesday, November 5, 1913, when the sluices of the Owens Valley aqueduct opened and chief engineer William Mulholland modestly inaugurated this modern miracle with five little words, "There it is! Take it!"

Recalling the dramatic event with a touch of regret, the *Laconic* noted:

If the day had been made to order the climatic conditions could not have been improved upon. True, it was a little warm, but that was the cause of the magnificent day. It was a great occasion, but the crowd failed to measure up with such an event. It was a celebration that will not occur again in the history of the southern country, but the people stayed

home and howled that the water would never get here. The crowd should have been twice as large. Even the city of Los Angeles would not close their schools.

The opening of the big gates on that aqueduct and the rushing of the waters down that steep cascade was a grand and awe-inspiring sight and should have been witnessed by the schoolchildren who in later years would be able to see the marvelous transformation that these waters will work in Southern California.

Like water, optimism flowed unbounded. In 1914 the Businessmen's Association was expanded to become the Lankershim Chamber of Commerce. No other organization in the town's history proved to be as influential. It served as a kind of unofficial city council, and the votes taken in the chamber over the next few years virtually sealed Lankershim's future. A significant number of service, professional, and social organizations were also formed around this time, including the the Kiwanis Club, the Lankershim Women's Club, and the Rotary Club.

Spurred by a dynamic chamber of commerce, the hard-driving editorials of the *Laconic,* and the dramatic growth of the city of Los Angeles, the future of Lankershim seemed to be filled with fantastic possibilities.

Goin' Hollywood

1 9 1 5   t o   1 9 2 8

Early in 1915, at the southeast corner of Lankershim township, the finishing touches were being added to what the Universal Film Manufacturing Company called "the Wonder City of the World," the largest and most modern facility designed expressly for the production of motion pictures. Across the country at theaters showing Universal films, posters cried:

Aw, c'mon out!

Are you going to come on out to Universal City on March 15th or not? Are you going to give old Dull Care a kick in the shins, or are you going to stick around the old place and look glum?

See how slapstick comedies are made. See how big serials are produced. See your favorite screen stars do their work. See how the scenic artists put old Dame Nature to shame. See the cowboys, Indians and soldiers at their best or worst.

See how we have to use the brains God gave us in every conceivable way in order to MAKE THE PEOPLE LAUGH OR CRY OR SIT ON THE EDGE OF THEIR CHAIRS THE WORLD OVER!

C'mon out! Aw, c'mon!

Three years earlier the Universal Film Manufacturing Company, organized by German immigrant Carl Laemmle (pronounced *lem-ly*), was among the companies experimenting with Southern California filmmaking. Los Angeles' spectacular Mediterranean climate, snowcapped San Gabriel Mountains, Mojave desert, Pacific Ocean, and San Fernando Valley flatlands were far more reliable and scenic than the weather and locations around New York City, at that time the capital of the "flicker" industry.

In 1913 Laemmle already had three makeshift studios flourishing in Hollywood, but he recognized the advantages of merging his operations. As a result, Laemmle instructed his West Coast general manager, Isadore "Bernie" Bernstein, to look for a site on which Universal could build a permanent studio with the most up-to-date facilities.

Bernstein was at first attracted to the Oak Ridge Ranch, a horse-breeding spread along the northeastern edge of Cahuenga Pass. Universal leased part of the property and erected a few small buildings. But with box-office revenues at an all-time high and theater owners demanding more and better movies, in March 1914 Bernstein made a $3,500 down payment on a total purchase price of $165,000 for 230 acres of the adjoining Taylor Ranch.

Soon, cartloads of sets, cameras, and other equipment began arriving at the new location for filming of the westerns that Laemmle and the public craved. As a boy growing up in Europe, Laemmle had become enamored of Westerns by reading American dime novels, and stories of the West continued to fascinate him and the movie-going public.

Laemmle considered Bernstein's San Fernando Valley location ideal for

The banner, "Universal Welcomes You," greets all visitors to the then young Universal City Studios around 1920. Copyright © by Universal Pictures, a Division of Universal City Studios, Inc. Courtesy of MCA Publishing Rights, a Division of MCA Inc.

Western filmmaking. It was, after all, the real thing! Laemmle was also intrigued by the fact that the ranch was adjacent to the historic Campo de Cahuenga site.

Several of Laemmle's competitors, however, thought that locating a new studio so far from Hollywood was a gaffe of epic proportions. They said that Laemmle had spent $165,000 for scenery that could be filmed for free across large chunks of Southern California. Executives at other studios laughed and called it "Laemmle's Folly." Even Laemmle himself was reported to say, "I hope I didn't make a mistake coming out here." Some 75 years later, however, his choice proved to be prophetic. Universal City is today the world's oldest motion-picture studio located on its original site.

In June 1914 ground was officially broken. While construction continued, picture-making began. Later that year, even before the official opening, Universal City's first feature, *Damon and Pythias*, opened across the country. The weekend before the gates officially opened, a special Santa Fe train from Chicago carrying Laemmle and scores of celebrities, including Buffalo Bill Cody, arrived in Los Angeles.

On opening-day morning, March 15, 1915, 10,000 people jammed the roads leading to the new studio's gates on Lankershim Boulevard. Laura Oakley, one of Universal's biggest stars and the chief of the new city's police department, presented a golden key to Laemmle, who unlocked the gates and inaugurated the festivities. The band played "The Star-Spangled Banner," the American flag was hoisted, and Laemmle led a thousand-strong sing-a-long of "I Love You, California."

A studio zoo housed dogs, cats, sheep, mules, monkeys, parrots, an elephant, and hundreds of horses and

for a crash into Mount Cahuenga. In a futile effort to save himself, Stites jumped from his plane without a parachute while Laemmle and a throng of dignitaries watched in horror. Though Stites managed to escape a fiery crash into the mountainside, his fall proved fatal, and the ceremonies came to an abrupt end. Stites is believed to be the first person to lose his life while performing motion-picture stunt work.

Despite the freak accident, civic pride in Lankershim received a sharp boost from what Laemmle unashamedly advertised as "the Strangest City in the World." Then, as now, the motion-picture business was regarded as exciting and glamorous, and the residents of Lankershim were thrilled to be a part of the world's largest and most-modern movie studio.

cattle. Universal City also had its own post office, hospital, restaurant, and fire department. All day long, crowds surged along mile-long Carl Laemmle Boulevard, the centerpiece of the new municipality.

The main attractions were a 300-by-50-foot main stage, which could accommodate up to five productions simultaneously, and a second stage that measured 200 feet by 50 feet. Viewing stands erected opposite the stages for the first time permitted the public to see how movie magic was created, and they were filled with some of the 20,000 visitors who jammed the new "city" on its first afternoon.

The personable "Uncle Carl," as Laemmle was called by practically everyone in the movie business because he hired so many of his relatives, believed that admitting the public brought him millions of dollars in free, word-of-mouth publicity. He figured that at least a hundred people heard about filmmaking from just one visitor to Universal City. Until the introduction of sound equipment in the late 1920s precluded the presence of noisy crowds, admission to Universal and a box lunch cost 25 cents.

On the second afternoon of the planned week-long festivities, tragedy struck. Frank Stites, a stunt pilot whose daredevil flying for the cameras had thrilled the crowd all morning, headed into a severe downdraft and straight

Lankershim continued to grow during the 1910s, though development slowed somewhat with America's entry into the "Great War." In 1916 a gas line made candles practically obsolete. As it did throughout the world, the postwar influenza pandemic hit Lankershim hard, and there were many deaths. Nevertheless, in 1920, the population reached 2,372, almost triple the 1910 total, and homeowners were asked to put street numbers on their residences to avoid confusion.

In 1921 a Lankershim landmark was created when Jim Wilson, who in 1932 became the Valley's first Los Angeles city councilman, sold his retailing business on Lankershim Boulevard to Hall and Ted Rathbun. The newly christened department store served as a magnet for the street, and soon an appealing array of high-fashion stores opened there. The Blue Bird Café became a popular hangout, as did the ice-cream parlor. For the first time, people complained about traffic congestion and inadequate parking. The town even had its own telephone exchange, and "Hello, Central?" became a familiar sound on the hand-cranked phones.

By the following year 25 streetcars and 17,000 automobiles made their way each day over Cahuenga Pass.

RIGHT: The grand set for the 1922 Universal production of Foolish Wives is shown here under contruction. Erich von Stroheim directed and starred in this lively tale of intrigue. Courtesy, Marc Wanamaker/Bison Archives

BELOW RIGHT: The charming Pacific Electric station and green at Chandler and Lankershim boulevards, pictured here in 1919, also served as the site for many town concerts and events. Courtesy, Weddington Family Collection

FACING PAGE: Looking north from the Hollywood Hills around 1917, the developing town of Lankershim can be seen next to Lankershim Boulevard, which runs at an angle to the northwest. Vineland Avenue cuts across Lankershim, with Ventura Boulevard visible running horizontally in the foreground. Courtesy, Weddington Family Collection

With all the changes, the town began to develop an interest in its history. In 1923 Mrs. Armitage S.C. Forbes and other preservation-minded activists persuaded the City of Los Angeles to acquire the Campo de Cahuenga site for $15,000. A monument containing the words of Mrs. Jesse Benton Frémont was erected to her husband, and Andrés Pico was honored in a similar memorial.

While one historic landmark reappeared, one of Lankershim Boulevard's most famous sights fell victim to development. The 300 cattle of the Hartsook dairy ranch were moved to their new home on Vineland Avenue. The land was now more valuable for housing than for grazing.

In the fall of 1923 the 152-acre Toluca Rancho was acquired for a real-estate subdivision around its spring-fed lake. Nearby, the 60-acre Charles Frieburg Ranch on the west and the Rollie Brown Ranch on the east were joined for the construction of the Lakeside Country Club. Silent-screen stars soon found Toluca Lake an appealing place for a home. Matinee idols Dick Arlen and Charlie Farrell were among the first notables to build their homes there; scores of others followed.

That same year, dusty Seventh Street was renamed Victory Boulevard in honor of World War I veterans, as a severe drought brought the water issue to the crisis point. The drilling of additional artesian wells had

caused the underground water pressure to drop, and wells had to be dug ever deeper. It became clear that to keep pace with its needs the town had to obtain a more abundant and reliable source of water.

The town was split between two options: joining the city of Los Angeles through annexation or becoming an independent city through incorporation under state law. A chamber of commerce fact-finding committee found that Lankershim's western neighbor, Van Nuys, was happy with its decision to join Los Angeles; to the east, the incorporated city of Burbank was satisfied with its independent status. While Lankershim anticipated a September 10th total eclipse of the sun and touted local movie star Rin-tin-tin (a stray dog found in Germany during the war), the town's 1,200 residents vigorously debated the choice.

A Committee of One Hundred, made up of the great majority of Lankershim's most influential citizens, came out strongly in favor of joining Los Angeles. Its full-page ads in the *Laconic* proclaimed, "Lankershim's destiny is bound up in the growth and development of Los Angeles." A rival Citizens Committee of 400, whose members remained anonymous, urged a no vote on annexation and supported the "as is" line in the special balloting set for Wednesday, October 31.

By August the *Laconic* wrote that the push for incorporation was virtually dead. "All idea or talk of incorporating the territory into a separate city government . . . has been dropped," it reported, "as it is felt that a city . . . would be too limited." The paper enthusiastically supported annexation. A controversial election-eve report that taxes would double with annexation heightened voters' emotions and made the outcome uncertain.

With a voter turnout of 85 percent, the results showed that both of the town's precincts approved annex-ation. The vote was 572 to 441. Within days, a unit of the city of Los Angeles fire department appeared, even though annexation would not become official until the close of business on the last day of the year.

About this time Lankershim also saw the chicken industry overtake the fruit business. The town now claimed to be the "Home of the Hen." Chicken coops be-came a common sight, and one henhouse was a mile long. Millions of eggs from Lankershim were shipped out annually. Even Universal City counted thousands of chickens among its inhabitants, and eggs were sold to the tourists as they left the studio.

It was the best of times, and town pride in Lanker-shim soared. Rathbun's, which seemed to be expanding constantly, advertised that it was holding a song contest in conjunction with the Kiwanis Club. The store pub-lished the best compositions in the *Lankershim Song Book*. Typical was an entry with lyrics set to the tune of "Yankee Doodle."

Lankershim's the place to live;
Lankershim's impressive;
Lankershim's the home of the peach;
Lankershim's progressive.

On July 1, 1926, construction crews finished a new roadway over Cahuenga Pass. It marked the first use of county gas-tax funds on a city street. Nevertheless, with the opening on September 30, 1926, of El Portal Theater, located on the site of the original Weddington ranch, hometown moviegoers were spared the trip to Hollywood. The 1,800-seat, fireproof, state-of-the-art theater cost a whopping $250,000 and proved to be a first-rate cultural and architectural addition.

New-construction figures continued to break records in 1927, and the area was unquestionably the fastest-growing community in the Valley and near the top of the list for the county. An impressive half-million-dollar high school was about to open at Magnolia Boulevard and Colfax Avenue and serve as a powerful lure for new residents. No longer would a daily commute to Hollywood High be necessary for hundreds of schoolchildren. A new Women's Club headquarters opened, and an art-deco, county-wide headquarters was planned by the Southern California Gas Company.

A bond proposal for a new park on the northeast side of Tujunga Wash was proposed for the next election. The $378,000 needed to cover the purchase of the parkland would come from 30 annual tax installments levied against local property owners in a park assessment district. The vote was seen as a test of the community's character. It was said that rural areas such as Lankershim didn't need a park, yet no one could deny that new construction was causing the countryside to disappear rapidly.

Almost everywhere, farmland and orchards were giving way to new homes and offices. Lankershim even boasted of the first traffic signal in the Valley. Located at the intersection of Ventura Highway (now Ventura Boulevard) and Lankershim Boulevard, the device joined 133 others in the transmountain part of the city. Its $1,250 cost would be paid by its violators. Offering an alternative to the vanishing countryside, the Women's Club sponsored "Plant a Tree Week."

As had become the custom, the park proposal was

virtually unanimously supported by an array of influential civic groups that included the chamber of commerce, the realty board, the Kiwanis, the Rotary, and the Women's Club, as well as the Parent-Teacher Association. Newspaper ads promoted the fact that the park would replace "unsightly campgrounds."

In January 1927, 1,171 voters cast their ballots on the park-bond measure, which required a two-thirds majority for approval. Split 800 to 371, the voters approved the measure by only 18 votes. Lankershim Park (now North Hollywood Park) became the largest public green space in the Valley. In the next few years, it would include a regional branch of the City of Los Angeles Public Library, tennis courts, playing fields, and a swimming pool.

On June 21 of that milestone year, the Lankershim *Press* (as the old *Laconic* was now called) broke the news that the Central Motion Picture District, a corporation set up to develop movie-company sites, had arranged for the construction of a $20-million film center named Studio City. The development was planned for the northeast corner of Ventura Highway and Prospect Street (now Laurel Canyon Boulevard).

The first phase of the new addition would be the construction of the 200-acre Mack Sennett studio. (In 1935 it became the Republic Pictures Studio and later the CBS/MTM Studio.) The mission-style administration building would be two stories tall, to rank it among the highest structures in the Valley. The white stucco studio frontage would be 100 feet by 425 feet.

The new stages would be the most modern in the world, even more advanced than the ones in Universal City, already 12 years old. The public was so excited about the news of the gigantic new studio that an estimated 100,000 cars toured the site the next weekend.

The announcement for the new studio placed its location in North Hollywood, which Universal City had lately also applied to itself. The town of Lankershim went unmentioned in newspaper reports all over the world. All of the publicity about the gigantic Studio City project identified it as being in

North Hollywood.

The world, it seemed, was entranced with the Hollywood name, and picture makers refused to lose that identification by locating in the Valley. Guy Weddington, the president of the chamber of commerce, ordered that a committee be formed to test public sentiment for a change of name. A petition to the postmaster general was available for signing at the chamber of commerce. In a front-page editorial the *Press* promoted the idea of a name change for the entire district:

By co-operating with these builders and bringing the mighty magic name of Hollywood into this section, a period of development and prosperity will settle over this section never before witnessed. These capitalists and picture magnates do not want to lose the name of Hollywood, and all their transactions and publicity has to do with North Hollywood.

If the change is not made, Lankershim will be lost and ignored as a place on the map. The new developers will out-

shadow the development done in the immediate vicinity by their North Hollywood publicity. United, the whole district will advance under one banner—North Hollywood. Then in a few years, it will all melt into a greater Hollywood with the "north" prefix disappearing.

When word was leaked at a chamber of commerce meeting that the studio chiefs were indeed determined to

ABOVE: The bustling community of North Hollywood can be seen in this 1927 view, looking south along Lankershim Boulevard at Chandler Boulevard. The town boasted the first traffic signal erected in the San Fernando Valley. Courtesy, Weddington Family Collection

LEFT: These hardy orchard workers pick the ripe fruit of heavily laden peach trees during Lankershim harvesttime in the early 1920s. Courtesy, Weddington Family Collection

FACING PAGE: Prominent citizen and civic leader of North Hollywood, Guy M. Weddington served as president of the chamber of commerce in 1927, led a bond drive for a community park, and was instrumental in improving Cahuenga Pass in the 1930s. Courtesy, Weddington Family Collection

This circa 1920 panoramic view of the San Fernando Valley was taken from the grade that is now part of Laurel Canyon Boulevard. Courtesy, Seaver Center for Western History Research, Natural History Museum of Los Angeles County

keep their industry under the Hollywood label, regardless of where facilities were actually located, and would not mention Lankershim, a change of name became irresistible.

Opposition to the proposal was almost nonexistent. Universal City also supported the move to rename the whole area North Hollywood. A reported 90 percent of Lankershim residents signed the petition, and on August 15, 1927, the post office officially recognized the town's third name. Like a new movie star discarding an old name in order to appear more attractive, in only 31 years the lonely frontier town of Toluca had become the thriving, motion-picture glamour capital of North Hollywood.

That year also marked a turning point for the motion-picture industry, as Warner Brothers suddenly and unexpectedly introduced sound in their Al Jolson movie, *The Jazz Singer.* "You ain't heard nothin' yet"—a line of dialogue from the picture—became a national catchphrase.

At first, Laemmle regarded the introduction of spoken dialogue as a fad and felt that the public would soon tire of "the talkies," as movies with soundtracks were derisively called.

Universal had produced several of the most popular silent films, and Laemmle was therefore slow to convert to sound. Lon Chaney, as the horribly deformed bell-ringer Quasimodo, had thrilled audiences around the world in the studio's 1923 version of *The Hunchback of Notre Dame.* Under the supervision of 24-year-old Irving Thalberg, Universal's head of production and Laemmle's former personal assistant, an exact duplicate of the medieval Paris cathedral was built on the back lot and became an incongruous landmark beneath Mount Cahuenga.

In 1925, the studio followed up its *Hunchback* success by also casting the so-called Man of a Thousand Faces in the title role of *The Phantom of the Opera.* The production's huge five-tiered opera-house set was reported to seat 3,000 extras, many from Lankershim.

Westerns that stressed hard-riding cowboys had also become a Universal staple, as Hoot Gibson (directed by a young John Ford) and Tom Mix galloped over the nearby hills and contributed further evidence to Laemmle's theory that he could wait out the sound

LEFT: *Pictured center with his trusty megaphone, Rupert Julian directs the cast of Universal's 1925 production of* Phantom of the Opera. *Courtesy, Marc Wanamaker/ Bison Archives*

BELOW: *Universal Pictures was a booming film company by the 1930s, a fact in which North Hollywood residents took great pride. Copyright © Universal Pictures, a Division of Universal City Studios, Inc. Courtesy of MCA Publishing Rights, a Division of MCA Inc.*

FACING PAGE: *The 200-acre Mack Sennett Studio (now the site of today's CBS/MTM facility) is pictured here under construction at the corner of Laurel Canyon and Ventura boulevards in 1928. Note the fruit orchards behind the studio just across the Los Angeles River. Courtesy, Studio City Chamber of Commerce*

frenzy. Touting his earlier achievements, Laemmle felt that introducing English-language dialogue to such films would cost him sizable chunks of his huge overseas markets and unnecessarily complicate the distribution of what he regarded as a "universal" product.

Of all the major studios, Universal was the slowest to convert to sound, but by the end of the 1920s, however, it became clear even to Uncle Carl that a new era had begun and that if Universal City was to keep pace with the other studios, it would have to convert to sound.

On December 2, 1928, Universal officially released its first 100-percent talkie, *Melody of Love,* starring Walter Pidgeon. The following year it added newly recorded songs to the silent footage it had already filmed of the Broadway musical *Show Boat.*

Although the new movie "soundstages" and microphones effectively barred the public from the movie sets and the studio tour was abandoned (until it was revived in 1964), Universal City—like its newly renamed neighbor, North Hollywood—was poised for the 1930s and a decade that promised new heights of unparalleled prosperity.

America's Fastest-Growing Community

1929 to 1945

A s 1929 began, North Hollywood's pioneer era was clearly over. The issues associated with modern city living were multiplying as fast as tract housing. Inadequate roads, overcrowding in public schools, insufficient mass transportation, a water shortage, a Mediterranean fruit-fly infestation, child molestations, political corruption, drunk drivers, suicides, a high crime rate, and illicit drugs were all front-page news stories in the North Hollywood *Press*. The Boy Scout troop and the Girl Scout troop joined to condemn the use of healthful-looking youths in cigarette ads.

Stock brokers and economists predicted that the boom of the 1920s would continue. Mother's Day brought the opening of a new shopping center in Toluca Lake. North Hollywood Park was set to expand its facilities with the opening of the branch library and had solicited bids for the construction of a swimming pool. The good life, it seemed, was still getting better.

The chamber of commerce organized a cleanup day with the goal of ridding North Hollywood of weeds and other "unsightly spots." There was talk of digging a Laurel Canyon tunnel to help alleviate the heavy traffic over Cahuenga Pass. The opening of the Grand Central Air Terminus, just across the city line in Burbank, and news of Boeing's move into the area inspired the North Hollywood *Press* to predict that the area would become the aircraft industry's "Detroit of the West."

But the nation's economy suffered a severe shock from the stock-market crash of October 1929. It was said that Guy Weddington's hair turned white overnight, but a mostly cavalier North Hollywood public opinion held that California and the West could escape any economic damage caused by Wall Street and Eastern bankers.

The North Hollywood *Press* commented on the income from 1929's Christmas shopping season: "Business is good, and all signs point to continued prosperity in 1930. Less caviar was served at some Christmas dinners and pâté de foie gras was absent from several menus. But there were several hundred thousand more Americans with a few billions more to spend than there were at this time last year."

Nevertheless, by the middle of January 1930, the *Press* was much more concerned that the recent economic troubles would not leave as suddenly as they had arrived: "Today, 40 men and as many women are listed [on the unemployment rolls] for work, and not one call has been received all week for any sort of employment. Everyone in the U.S. cannot expect to come out to North Hollywood and find jobs." The town's population reached 19,352 in the 1930 census.

Despite an overriding concern about the national economy, local issues continued to stir heavy interest. Many Lankershim Boulevard merchants grew

Expansion of civic services to meet the needs of a growing population was just one of the many challenges facing North Hollywood as it advanced into the 1930s. Leading community citizens participated in this tree-planting event at Vineland Avenue and Burbank Boulevard around 1932. This local beautification project was sponsored by the North Hollywood Women's Club. Courtesy, Universal City—North Hollywood Chamber of Commerce

restless over what they considered their street's anachronistic name. The town of Lankershim had become North Hollywood, and they sought a similar rechristening for their street.

Yet a move to rename the thoroughfare North Hollywood Boulevard was rejected when the consensus of the community decided that people were having enough trouble distinguishing between the communities of North Hollywood and Hollywood. Similarly changing the name of the boulevard, it was felt, would only compound the confusion. People complained that mail and telephone calls were misdirected because of the overlap in town nomenclatures. The *Press* and the chamber of commerce appealed to residents not to abbreviate North Hollywood with N. Hollywood or—even worse—No. Hollywood.

Toluca Lake was gaining popularity with the movie colony and even began to threaten Beverly Hills' reputation as the home of the stars. Oliver Hardy, Sophie Tucker, Bob Hope, Bing Crosby, William S. Hart, and Noah Beery were some of the Hollywood stars to buy homes there.

Amelia Earhart, the first woman to fly the Atlantic solo and an aviatrix who earned a worldwide reputation for the Lockheed planes she flew out of Burbank, also became one of Toluca Lake's most famous residents. Active in the North Hollywood community while a student at the University of Southern California in 1928, Earhart's endearing smile and tousled hair became familiar sights around town.

The house that Earhart shared with her husband, publisher and publicist George Putnam, became a tourist mecca, and even those whom she had never met were greatly saddened when she vanished over the Pacific in July 1937 on an around-the-world flight. Several months after Earhart's mysterious disappearance, the North Hollywood Jaycees erected a plaque in her honor at 5 Corners—where Lankershim Boulevard meets the intersection of Vineland Avenue and Camarillo Street—itself the site of many a fatal automobile accident.

Almost two years after the Wall Street crash, news items in the local press reflected the view that merely displaying a positive attitude could make the Depression go away. Real-estate sales were a key economic indicator, and when 10 acres at Cahuenga and Camarillo were sold for a new subdivision, the *Press* wrote that the transaction "sounded the death knell to the pessimistic atmosphere that has been prevailing for some time. The bottom evidently has been touched and prospects again have a brighter outlook." But still the Depression lingered.

Benefits for the unemployed and homeless were held at El Portal Theater, and the Community Chest and the Family Welfare Association campaigned for donations. The North Hollywood Joy Club was formed; it attempted to beat old man Depression and turn adversity into opportunity by creating an atmosphere of cheerfulness. Each member pledged to wear a huge

ABOVE: Believe it or not these three men were photographed standing on the vast expanse of land that is now the site of the Sears, Roebuck and Company store at Laurel Canyon and Victory boulevards. Promoted as a great place to build a home, this land was being sold for development in 1933. Courtesy, Universal City—North Hollywood Chamber of Commerce

FACING PAGE, BOTTOM: North Hollywood's float entry titled the "Merry Wives" won second place in the 1938 Pasadena Tournament of Roses. Courtesy, Universal City—North Hollywood Chamber of Commerce

FACING PAGE, TOP: The first woman to make a solo flight across the Atlantic Ocean (1932), world-renowned Amelia Earhart captured the public's love and imagination with her daring and romantic approach to flying. A prominent resident of North Hollywood's Toluca Lake, Earhart vanished over the Pacific Ocean in 1937 during her attempted round-the-world flight. A statue was dedicated in her honor at North Hollywood Park on January 22, 1971, and the name of North Hollywood's library was changed to the Amelia Earhart Branch in 1980, reflecting the admiration the community still holds for this valiant heroine. Courtesy, Marjorie Roye Balas

button inscribed with the slogan "We Smile to Win."

Over 500 Christmas baskets were collected for the unemployed. The North Hollywood Chamber of Commerce became the headquarters for the entire San Fernando Valley's welfare-relief efforts, and in the 1932 election the North Hollywood Chamber of Commerce's first president, Jim Wilson, became the first city council member from the San Fernando Valley.

On August 1, 1933, the new Roosevelt Administration's controversial National Recovery Act (NRA) went into effect amid much fanfare. The NRA's distinctive blue eagle symbol, with the gears of industry in its left talon and bolts of lightning in its right, began to appear in North Hollywood stores, businesses, and homes as evidence of support for increased employment, a shorter workweek, and lower prices.

"It is the NEW ERA," the *Press* wrote enthusiastically. Within a few months, however, critics condemned the NRA's quasi-military regimentation as unlawful, and enthusiasm started to evaporate. The country's economic and political crisis deepened months later when the U.S. Supreme Court decided that the NRA was unconstitutional.

Up on "the Hill," as Universal City's neighbors called it, Carl Laemmle's regime was facing hard times. Under the supervision of his son, Carl Laemmle, Jr., who took over as head of production in 1929 following Irving Thalberg's defection to Louis B. Mayer's company, Universal had begun the 1930s with a prestigious version of the powerful antiwar drama, *All Quiet on the Western Front.*

At the third annual Academy Awards on April 30, 1930, *All Quiet* won three Oscars, including the award for Best Picture. In addition to earning the studio a healthy profit, the $1.2-million picture elevated Universal to a lofty status as a first-class film factory. One reviewer said of it, "The League of Nations could make no better investment than to buy the

Pictured here in the 1940s, the current North Hollywood Post Office on Chandler Boulevard opened on October 17, 1936. Courtesy, San Fernando Valley Historical Society

master print, reproduce it in every nation to show every year until the word 'war' is taken out of the dictionary."

Not so highfalutin was the slew of popular and now-classic horror films that the studio churned out in the early and mid-1930s. The granddaddy of them all was 1931's *Dracula*, with Hungary's Bela Lugosi playing the blood-sucking vampire count of Transylvania.

Frankenstein, with British actor Boris Karloff playing the mad doctor's oversized monster, followed in 1932, as did *The Mummy* and *The Murders in the Rue Morgue. The Invisible Man* (1933), *The Bride of Frankenstein* (1935), and *The Werewolf of London* (1935) were also successful and kept the company afloat, although just barely.

By November 1935, however, it became clear that Laemmle Jr.'s movies were costing more money than they were earning, and Laemmle Sr. was compelled to hock the studio to producer Charles Rogers and British moneyman John Cheever Cowdin. In an unsuccessful attempt to stave off new management, the elder Laemmle

put all his chips on a remake of *Show Boat.*

Unfortunately for the five-foot-two visionary of Cahuenga Pass, production difficulties, delays, and cost overruns doomed his effort, and on March 14, 1936—almost exactly 21 years to the day after the opening of the Universal City facility—the mortgagees exercised their rights. Laemmle and his son were out. Financially secure nevertheless, the pioneering studio chief enjoyed an active retirement from his home in Beverly Hills until his death three years later.

In 1936 the current North Hollywood post office opened on land donated by the Weddington family, and the new facility opened to great fanfare on October 17. The new San Fernando Valley *Times* assumed control of the North Hollywood *Press,* although it promised to maintain the community's sense of identity by publishing a North Hollywood edition.

Further evidence of suburbanization could be found in the fact that an ultramodern apartment building of 30 units was scheduled for construction on Laurel Canyon Boulevard. Along Lankershim Boulevard, retail sales at Christmas were estimated to be back at the pre-Depression level.

In 1937 the Southern California Automobile Club published a report that advocated the construction of an elaborate system of new "motorways" that would provide

LEFT AND BELOW: The devastating storm and ensuing flood of 1938 took some 49 lives in the San Fernando Valley and caused millions of dollars in damage. Thanks to the clear-headed thinking of the chamber of commerce president, Ted Rathbun, the Army Corps of Engineers was called in to help prevent even worse destruction of the hard-hit North Hollywood area. Courtesy, Weddington Family Collection

of the bridges over the river had been swept away, and the federal Works Projects Administration immediately began building new ones. Construction crews on the crucial Lankershim Boulevard bridge worked round-the-clock.

The final count of storm-related Valley deaths reached 49, with property damage hitting $40 million. Millions of dollars in claims were filed against the city. (The claims were later rejected on the basis that the deluge and its damage were caused by "an act of God," not municipal negligence.) In May, federal and state agencies superseded the voters' earlier rejection of a crucial flood-control project and ordered the imme-

high-speed roads without stoplights, similar to the autobahns that linked major German cities. Soon, the state was planning such a road to relieve the constant traffic bottlenecks on Cahuenga Pass.

On Wednesday morning, March 2, 1938, a storm of epic proportions inundated North Hollywood with a torrential downpour that transformed the usually tranquil Los Angeles River and Tujunga Wash into raging killers. By 3:30 that afternoon, flood-ravaged refugees began assembling in the North Hollywood High School gymnasium, as radio station KFWB broadcast the names of the missing.

That day, seven survivors of the great disaster were pulled from Tujunga Wash while would-be rescuers watched in horror as four victims were swept away and drowned. Every available blanket from local stores was requisitioned, while the chamber of commerce served as the emergency-relief headquarters.

The rain continued throughout the week, and by the time the storm had passed, 11 inches of rain had fallen in five days. More than 100 police were called in to search for victims. Lankershim Boulevard shops were filled with several inches of mud. Trucks and tractors were brought in to remove the tons of debris created by the storm. The following Saturday, North Hollywood was placed under martial law to prevent looting. Most

BELOW: Attendance at North Hollywood High reached 1,639 students when this photograph was taken in 1939—the same year World War II began in Europe. Courtesy, Weddington Family Collection

RIGHT: This stunning aerial view looking north to the San Gabriel Mountains shows the rapid growth North Hollywood had experienced by 1941. Laurel Canyon Boulevard runs north and south in the center of the photograph, across Ventura Boulevard and the Los Angeles River. Courtesy, Universal City— North Hollywood Chamber of Commerce

diate construction of Hansen Dam.

By summer almost all the damage had been repaired, and a semblance of normality returned. A new dial telephone system created temporary chaos because everybody's phone numbers had to be changed. New telephone subscribers signed up at the rate of 100 a month, serving as dramatic testimony to the town's phenomenal growth.

A shrewd civic publicity campaign that would spread North Hollywood's fame across the nation began with the selection of curvaceous film starlet Glenda Farrell as North Hollywood's first honorary mayor. Universal City capped its remodeling efforts by announcing the construction of a new six-story administration building, the tallest structure in the Valley and widely regarded as the area's first "skyscraper."

The new building reflected the studio's modest successes, primarily a string of Deanna Durbin pictures, starting with 1937's *One Hundred Men and a Girl*. Durbin, a wholesome soprano who was Universal's answer to Judy Garland, won a loyal following and became one of Universal's most bankable stars.

The confidence expressed by management's building program was borne out over the next seven years as Universal released a respectable number of box-office attractions, including *Destry Rides Again* (with James Stewart and Marlene Dietrich), *My Little Chickadee* (with Mae West and W.C. Fields), comedies that starred radio's popular Bud Abbott and Lou Costello, mysteries solved by Sherlock Holmes, spinoffs of Universal's previous horror movies including *The Invisible Woman* and *The Mummy's Tomb*, and the Flash Gordon serial, starring Olympic swimming champion Buster Crabbe.

In 1940 North Hollywood led the San Fernando Valley in construction permits at a time when the Valley was the fastest-growing area of its size in the United States. With Nazi armies on the march in Europe, Lockheed began to triple its output of war planes. Within 12 months it would more than triple its work force to almost 50,000 employees, many of whom lived across the

city line in North Hollywood.

A dramatic population influx caused by burgeoning defense plants in the area led to a housing shortage, but Studio City homeowners who were concerned about overdevelopment blocked the construction of a 12-unit apartment building. Suddenly, it seemed that there would be limits on development much sooner than most people had expected.

Increased traffic caused Cahuenga Pass to be widened into what the state highway department called "one of the most beneficial highway projects ever undertaken in the Los Angeles metropolitan area." On June 15, 1940, a ceremony near the Hollywood Bowl featured newly installed North Hollywood mayor Gene Autry and the mayors of Los Angeles, Sherman Oaks, and Burbank. A symbolic strip of motion-picture film was held across the road and then cut to inaugurate the 1.8-mile section. A gaggle of celebrities paraded Ford Model T's and other antique vehicles to the top of the hill, then back down to attend a luncheon at the Hollywood Bowl.

This $1.5-million first chunk in the Cahuenga Freeway inaugurated the new eight-lane highway as far as Mulholland Drive Bridge. With the Pacific Electric tracks running in the middle of the new road and a traffic underpass that went southeast under the tracks, the project was considered an elaborate example of ultramodern vehicular engineering. A second section of the so-called Cahuenga Freeway that extended the roadway as far as Barham Road (formerly known as Dark Canyon) was opened in December 1940.

Experimental television station W6XAO announced the construction of a powerful new transmitter atop the mountain adjacent to Cahuenga Pass in anticipation of its being licensed for commercial broadcasting on September 1, 1940. Its mountaintop transmitter was expected to provide North Hollywood and other Valley homes with some of the best television reception in the world. But television broadcasting was to be severely curtailed for the next five years as the war complicated station licensing.

As the crisis in Europe intensified, North Hollywood and the rest of the Valley began to assume a position of national importance as a production center for

military materiel. A superhighway along the Los Angeles River was envisioned to run from Van Nuys to the harbor at San Pedro and promoted as vital in the event of war. North Hollywood men registered for the draft.

The virtually unthinkable occurred on December 7, 1941, when a pleasant Sunday morning was shattered by radio news bulletins announcing that Japanese bombers had mounted a devastating attack on the U.S. Pacific Fleet at Pearl Harbor. Ironically, Europe had been everyone's preoccupation. Immediately, there was anxiety that Japan would next attack defense plants along the coast and in the nearby San Fernando Valley.

North Hollywood residents were advised by the government to avoid hysteria but to report any suspicious behavior to the Federal Bureau of Investigation. To prevent sabotage, the Owens River aqueduct was placed under 24-hour guard within three hours of the attack on Pearl Harbor. Additional guards were hired at $5.50 per day. All dams, bridges, power stations, and tunnels

in the area were also provided with extra protection. Scores of men and women volunteered to serve as air-raid wardens and auxiliary police.

By the middle of December 1941, news was received of the first North Hollywood casualties. Four local boys who grew up in the same neighborhood and who enlisted in the navy at the same time had perished during the initial Japanese attack.

At night the rumblings of military convoys could be heard along major roads throughout the Valley. Powerful antiaircraft guns were installed throughout North Hollywood. Interceptor planes were placed on alert. Experts assured Lockheed workers that their factory was completely camouflaged and prepared for any attack.

Valley-wide blackouts were ordered, and when the lights on the Lankershim Boulevard bridge over the Los Angeles River continued to burn one night, an investigation was ordered. Even the North

FACING PAGE: An increase in traffic through the Cahuenga Pass resulted in the building of the first link of the Cahuenga Freeway, known today as the Hollywood Freeway. Pictured here under construction in 1940, the state highway department called this improvement "one of the most beneficial highway projects ever undertaken in the Los Angeles metropolitan area." Note the Pacific Electric tracks that would run down the middle of the completed highway. Courtesy, Department of Special Collections, University Research Library, UCLA

ABOVE: Able-bodied men throughout the North Hollywood area were recruited for the armed forces as the war in Europe intensified. Courtesy, Universal City—North Hollywood Chamber of Commerce

Within a few months, as the threat of a mainland attack decreased, the Los Angeles Chamber of Commerce stressed the Valley's remoteness from enemy territory and its resulting immunity from an assault. The organization commissioned a map showing that Southern California was farther away from Germany and Japan than anywhere else in the continental United States: Even Kansas City, it showed, was closer to Berlin than North Hollywood was to Tokyo.

The rationing of tires and gasoline led to carpooling; travelers who were more exercise-minded took to bicycles. Toluca Lake celebrities—including Bob Hope, Rudy Vallee, Red Skelton, and Bing Crosby—began defense bond national tours, organized morale-boosting shows for the troops, and further popularized their hometown. A United Service Organization canteen was opened at 5252 Lankershim Boulevard, and the Farm Security Administration called for "good farmers" to harvest the crops of the Japanese-American gardeners who had been detained in remote campsites under army orders.

A Victory Garden was opened just west of the post office on Chandler Avenue, and the water department offered discounts on all similar efforts to increase the production of food. To cooperate with the government's campaign to conserve clothing, several companies lifted their prohibitions on women wearing men's slacks.

Thousands of soldiers bivouacked in North Hollywood Park. The California State Guard held maneuvers there, and the public was invited to observe the training. North Hollywood High became a Red Cross casualty station, with the boys' gym serving as an emergency surgery center.

At the Battle of Midway in June 1942, the tide began to turn against the Japanese, and North Hollywood claimed its first war hero: Lieutenant Jack Whidden, a graduate of the local high school and the pilot of a bomber that sank a Japanese destroyer at the height of

FACING PAGE: An integral part of America's World War II war machine, the Lockheed facilities in nearby Burbank were completely prepared for any attack following the December 1941 bombing of Pearl Harbor. North Hollywood Chamber of Commerce officials are seen here touring the Lockheed plant in 1943. Courtesy, Universal City—North Hollywood Chamber of Commerce

ABOVE: Local residents responded to the call for much-needed guards, air-raid wardens, and auxiliary police in the early 1940s, as Southern California prepared itself for a possible Japanese attack. These North Hollywood men signed up as fire guards at El Portal Theater on Lankershim Boulevard. Courtesy, Universal City—North Hollywood Chamber of Commerce

Hollywood High School met blackout requirements. The chamber of commerce once again served as crisis-management headquarters. Air-raid siren tests at noon became familiar sounds.

In the midst of the outrage over the sneak attack, however, the Valley *Times* urged a judicious policy toward Japanese-Americans. "American-born Japanese must get fair play," it editorialized. "Throughout the Valley are American-born Japanese as loyal as you and I and as resentful over this unwarranted attack. Let's not make their difficult position worse by heaping indignities on them for a setting not of their own choosing."

battle. His father, also a resident of North Hollywood who worked at a fighter-aircraft factory in Burbank, told the local newspaper, "I build 'em, and he sinks 'em."

In 1943 the Valley was publicized by the Gordon Jenkins song "San Fernando Valley" in a new record by Toluca Lake's own Bing Crosby, which was widely heard on radio stations and juke boxes across the country and which is still popular today:

Oh! I'm packin' my grip
And I'm leavin' today,

'Cause I'm takin' a trip
Cal-i-forn-i-a way.

I'm gonna settle down and never more roam
And make the San Fernando Valley my home.

Jenkins became North Hollywood's honorary mayor as a result of the national notoriety for the area generated by "San Fernando Valley," and the town became known informally as "Bingville" in tribute to the crooner.

Following the Allies' successful invasion of France's Normandy beaches on D-Day, North Hollywood civic leaders and workaday wage-earners began planning for the postwar economy. Optimism ran high, and a return to the grim days of the Depression was considered unlikely. A speaker at the North Hollywood Rotary Club predicted that Los Angeles would become the largest city in the United States as a result of the postwar boom. Labor unrest became all too common, however, and a union jurisdictional dispute brought violence to the motion-picture industry before its settlement returned the

LEFT: Contributing to the 1944 War Fund Campaign, chief of civilian defense for the San Fernando Valley, Martin E. Pollard, presents a $250 check to Nancy Welbourn, vice chairman of volunteer services for the American Red Cross. Looking on is Gurney Newlin, chairman of the Los Angeles Chapter of the American Red Cross. Courtesy, Universal City—North Hollywood Chamber of Commerce

FACING PAGE: Harry and Peggy McKim were just two of the many dedicated North Hollywood citizens who volunteered their time and effort to the war cause. The McKim children collected newspapers and magazines for the Civil Defense Committee in Action, whose motto was "in thought, in word, in action, be American." Courtesy, Universal City—North Hollywood Chamber of Commerce

BELOW: Aircraft-related industries experienced explosive growth during World War II and the ensuing postwar years. Employees of one such business, the local Schroeder Tool and Manufacturing Company, take a moment from making aircraft valves to smile for the camera. Courtesy, Universal City—North Hollywood Chamber of Commerce

studios to full production.

Virtually all businesses in North Hollywood closed in mourning following Franklin Delano Roosevelt's sudden death in April 1945, and on V-E (Victory in Europe) Day the following month, public sentiment decreed that no celebrations be held in recognition of the fact that the war was only half over and that Japan remained to be conquered. The best predictions were that it might take several more years for the Allies to finish the war.

During mopping-up operations in Germany, a North Hollywood officer supervised the uncovering of $100 million in gold bars that the Nazi leaders had hidden away in anticipation of their flight from the country to avoid capture. Back home, new weapons were frequently unveiled and became a popular topic of conversation. In August 1945 Lockheed unveiled its first jet fighter, the P-80 Shooting Star.

The biggest story of the war hit front pages all over the world in early August: the United States had detonated an atomic bomb over Hiroshima. In anticipation of Japan's surrender, North Hollywood retail-store advertisements announced plans to close on V-J (Victory in Japan) Day. California's alcohol-control board ordered that when that day came, no alcohol could be bought or sold anywhere in the state.

When the war finally ended, North Hollywood church bells could be heard in every neighborhood, and practically every street had a block party. Returning veterans by the thousands intended to settle in North Hollywood. Providing jobs, housing, roads, and schools for them became the new order of the day as the unprecedented postwar boom began.

A Peach of a Place for a Home

1 9 4 5   t o   t h e   P r e s e n t

Almost exactly 100 years after the first pioneer homes were pieced together along what is now Lankershim Boulevard, a glamorous new high-tech, state-of-the-art mini-city rises amid the low-rise buildings of the past. Named "The Academy" in honor of the Academy of Television Arts and Sciences that makes its home here, this 22-acre complex of office towers, retail stores, restaurants, apartments, and a luxury hotel marks the beginning of a North Hollywood renaissance that is almost 50 years in the making. This most recent chapter of North Hollywood history begins on V-J Day, August 14, 1945.

At the end of World War II, thousands of veterans returning from the Pacific sought to recapture for a lifetime the glimpse of the North Hollywood good life that they had seen here on their way to war. With the federal government offering generous mortgage loans to millions of returning GIs, hundreds of new homes sprang up each month on former sites of North Hollywood farms, chicken coops, and fruit groves. What had been "The Home of the Hen" and "The Home of the Peach" became known as "A Peach of a Place for a Home."

Signaling how much times had changed, the North Hollywood Chamber of Commerce for the first time discouraged any further population growth. Available housing was already scarce, and many longtime residents feared that the dramatic influx of new residents would further erode the old-time community spirit of first-name neighborliness.

The City of Los Angeles' first official postwar estimate was that North Hollywood's population of about 90,000 would triple in 50 years; in fact, the town attracted that many residents in only about a dozen years.

In 1946 the first of several significant postwar corporate changes occurred in Universal City. The parent company merged with the smaller International Pictures Corporation to form Universal-International Pictures Corporation. One of the new management's first moves was to remove from production the adventure serials and westerns that had been Universal staples since Laemmle's creation of the company.

During the immediate postwar years, a widely divergent quality of films emerged from the studio. As the result of a deal that allowed Universal to release British pictures made by the J. Arthur Rank company, the studio won its second Best Picture Oscar in 1948 for Laurence Olivier's version of William Shakespeare's *Hamlet*.

No film could have been more different than the belly-laugh comedies that the studio was making with Abbott and Costello, Francis the Talking Mule (which costarred in a popular series with Donald O'Connor), and the down-home Ma and Pa Kettle (played by Marjorie Main and Percy Kilbride).

Perhaps the best results for Universal, however, came in the chambers of the United States Supreme Court justices who ruled in 1949 that the major Hollywood studios were required to divest themselves of their theater chains.

The hustle and bustle of a prosperous North Hollywood can be seen here on Lankershim Boulevard in the 1950s. Courtesy, Universal City—North Hollywood Chamber of Commerce

FACING PAGE: Since its unveiling in 1971 the striking Amelia Earhart statue by artist Ernie Shelton has graced the landscaped grounds of North Hollywood Park. Photo by Patty Salkeld

ABOVE: Considered to be the best place to shop in the San Fernando Valley's booming postwar years, Lankershim Boulevard boasted Kirk's store—a fine menswear shop that catered to the well-dressed man. Courtesy, Universal City—North Hollywood Chamber of Commerce

Valley. Frequently the sidewalk crowds were so thick that little boys and girls were swept into the street, and a shortage of parking spaces became a major problem.

Rathbun's Department Store, which prided itself on a tradition of quality merchandise and attentive customer service, boasted the highest sales for a retail store with its square footage in the country. F.W. Woolworth and Company opened its largest five-and-dime store in the Valley on Lankershim Boulevard.

The affluence of the North Hollywood lifestyle was reflected every morning in the thousands of cars on the Cahuenga Freeway, increasingly choked with traffic. With almost 90,000 vehicles scaling the road every day, it became the state's most heavily traveled throughfare, surpassing the Golden Gate Bridge.

The mid-century year began a decade in which the San Fernando Valley outgrew all other major urban areas in the country. Lloyds of London called the Valley "the fastest growing area in the world." The North Hollywood post office ranked as the 125th busiest out of 44,000 such outlets in the nation.

As North Hollywood absorbed so many newcomers, an awareness of the area's rich heritage increased. The San Fernando Valley Historical Society's efforts to restore the Campo de Cahuenga site reached fruition on November 8, 1950, when a replica of the original building was opened on Lankershim Boulevard opposite the main entrance to Universal City. Every January the historic signing of the Capitulation of Cahuenga is commemorated here with a colorful pageant that reflects the rancho days of the dons.

North Hollywood's flair for patriotism and community spirit was also depicted in the 1952 Tournament of Roses, when the town's "Betsy Ross and the Flag" float won first prize in its division. The North Hollywood beauty pageant sent its winning

Because Universal never had a theater chain, the upheavals resulting from the decision hurt that studio the least.

In 1950 Universal City added an additional 140 acres at the eastern end of the property and almost doubled the size of the back-lot area. The studio now stretched over 420 acres, making it not only the oldest motion-picture studio on its original site but also the largest film factory in the world. In 1952 corporate maneuverings enabled Decca Records to acquire 28 percent of Universal-International, a controlling interest.

As the first half of the century ended and postwar prosperity spread, Lankershim Boulevard regained its status as the San Fernando Valley's best and most popular place to shop. It became the major artery in the community that was the heart of the

ABOVE: Picturesque North Holly-wood Park is a central focus for local recreation and leisure-time activities. Photo by Patty Salkeld

RIGHT: North Hollywood High School continues to serve the challenging educational needs of the community. Photo by Patty Salkeld

North Hollywood's business district revitalization has taken shape in the form of the Academy of Television Arts and Sciences development project at the intersection of Lankershim and Magnolia boulevards. This six-phase development will feature more than one million square feet of prime office, retail, and restaurant space. Photo by Patty Salkeld

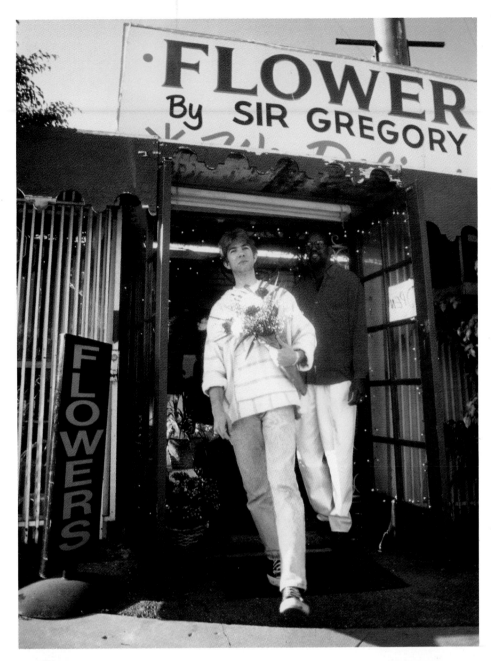

LEFT: Flowers by Sir Gregory is a fragrant and colorful oasis in the heart of North Hollywood. Photo by Patty Salkeld

FACING PAGE: A joint project between MCA and Texaco, the 36-story Universal City Plaza building stands as the tallest building in the San Fernando Valley. Texaco has been a major force in San Fernando Valley charitable activities, including the annual Charity Starscene, which is co-sponsored by the Universal City—North Hollywood Chamber of Commerce. Photo by Patty Salkeld

Considered to be the birthplace of California, the Campo de Cahuenga State Historic Park features a replica of the Feliz adobe where the Capitulation of Cahuenga was signed on January 13, 1847. This accord ended the Mexican-American War in California and was later formalized by the 1848 Treaty of Guadalupe Hidalgo. Photo by Patty Salkeld

Established by Nudie Cohn, the renowned clothing designer for country-western musicians and television and motion-picture celebrities, Nudie's is a North Hollywood landmark where one's taste for western attire can be satisfied. Photo by Patty Salkeld

LEFT: *Featuring the stars of the animated film classic in a full musical stage production at Universal Studios Hollywood,* An American Tail *transports visitors of all ages to the magical world of Fievel and his friends. Copyright © by Universal Pictures, a Division of Universal City Studios, Inc. Courtesy of MCA Publishing Rights, a Division of MCA, Inc.*

BELOW: *The world's first man-made 8.3 earthquake can be experienced by* Earthquake—The Big One *at Universal Studios Hollywood. Copyright © by Universal Pictures, a Division of Universal City Studios, Inc. Courtesy, of MCA Publishing Rights, a Division of MCA, Inc.*

girl to the Miss California contest.

In a quiet ceremony on March 4, 1952, in Studio City's quaint Little Brown Church in the Valley at 4418 Coldwater Canyon Boulevard, Universal-International actor Ronald Reagan (who had recently finished his work on "the Hill" in the comedy *Bedtime for Bonzo)* married Nancy Davis, a little-known actress from the same studio.

On December 29, 1952, competition from the automobile proved too much for the Pacific Electric's Big Red streetcars as the last of its kind trundled out of the Valley and up the center of Cahuenga Pass. The service to and from Hollywood was reportedly costing the Pacific Electric hundreds of thousands of dollars each year in operating losses. North Hollywood city councilman Jim Wilson worked with the local chamber of commerce and other influential civic groups for the continuation of the Big Reds, but the effort ultimately failed. Fred Weddington, who 41 years earlier had ridden the first Pacific Electric car to reach the town of Lankershim, was also aboard what local wags called "A Streetcar Named Expire."

At the northern end of town, a former cow pasture and the Tujunga Wash area near Victory Boulevard became the site of developer Bob Symonds' Valley Plaza, one of the nation's first regional shopping centers. With notable hyperbole, the center was promoted as "exceeding anything existing or planned anywhere else in the United States of similar character."

A gigantic $4-million Sears, Roebuck and Company store served as the center's anchor. The Sears store alone had more feet of counter space than any

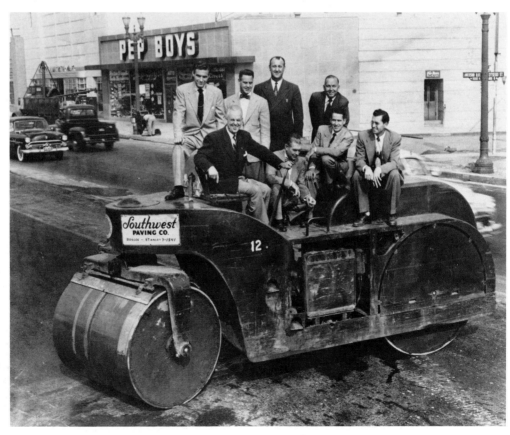

FACING PAGE: Overlooking Barham Boulevard and the Lakeside Country Club in December 1948, picturesque Toluca Lake is still a favorite North Hollywood neighborhood today. Courtesy, Universal City—North Hollywood Chamber of Commerce

ABOVE: Some of the San Fernando Valley's most important dignitaries were on hand for the retiring of the Pacific Electric's Big Red Valley line on December 29, 1952. Among those present were Fred Weddington, Martin E. Pollard, Mr. Whitsett, Monty Montana, and Ferdinand Mendenhall. Courtesy, Weddington Family Collection

other store west of Kansas City. Among the most up-to-date facilities in the store were "moving stairs." Almost 100 stores surrounded Valley Plaza's acres of free parking, and they served an estimated 100,000 shoppers a day.

On April 15, 1954, the California Department of Transportation opened the Hollywood Freeway's last stretch of road on Cahuenga Pass, a segment from Hollywood Boulevard to Mulholland Bridge. This revamped section of the former Cahuenga Freeway allowed a 10-minute commute from the center of North Hollywood through Whitley Heights and Echo Park to the Los Angeles Civic Center. At the same time, Vineland Avenue was widened to substitute for Lankershim Boulevard as a truck route.

The May Company Center (a major retail area now known as Laurel Plaza Shopping Center) opened on Laurel Canyon Boulevard in 1955 and combined with the nearby Valley Plaza to make that area of North Hollywood the largest regional shopping center west of the Mississippi. North Hollywood achieved a notable first in another category when its branch library was named the busiest in the United States.

In 1959 the Valley's United Chambers of Commerce presented their first annual Fernando Award to North Hollywood's Martin Pollard. This award, given to the Valley's most notable community-service volunteer, was won the next year by Russell Quisenberry (editor of the locally published Valley *Times*), who was also from North Hollywood. The Weddington family donated the land for North and South Weddington parks, and despite the newly transitory atmosphere created by apartment buildings and freeways, the town ended the decade much as it had begun—as one of the most rock-solid bedroom communities in Los Angeles.

At the same time, television was altering the basic economic structure of Universal City. By the start of the 1960s, the new medium's popularity caused moviegoing to drop by more than 5 million tickets from its 1957 level of 45 million admissions. As a result, fewer films were produced, and in many Universal City soundstages the silence was almost deafening. The studio's operating loss in 1958 was $2 million.

The following year a new buyer appeared on the scene: the Music Corporation of America (MCA), led by its founder and chairman, ophthalmologist Dr. Jules Stein, and its president, Lew Wasserman. Cash heavy as a result of its phenomenal successes with television productions, MCA paid $11.25 million for the 420 acres of Universal City, with the provision that it could lease whatever facilities it needed to film its TV shows.

The spicy (for 1959) Rock Hudson and Doris Day romantic comedy *Pillow Talk* became a suprise hit; the picture not only propelled Hudson and Day to the top of every Top-10 list of male and female Hollywood stars, it also spawned several equally successful cinematic clones, including *Lover Come Back* and *Send Me No Flowers*.

In 1960 the first section of the Ventura Freeway was opened with tremendous fanfare by Governor Edmund G. "Pat" Brown. Two years later, the Hollywood and the Golden State freeways were linked

very center of California.

In 1960 Universal released Stanley Kubrick's Roman epic *Spartacus*. Its $12-million cost made it the studio's most expensive production to date. Two years later, MCA completed its buy-out of Universal-International when it purchased Decca Records. The word *International* was dropped from the company's name, and Universal's fourth logo debuted in Alfred Hitchcock's *The Birds*.

Construction was started on a 14-story MCA executive tower as the studio entered its most successful era under the new management. *To Kill a Mockingbird*, released in 1963, became one of the most prestigious and respected films of the year.

when the Ventura Freeway cut through the Toluca Lake area. Also that year, the Hollywood Freeway was extended from Lankershim Boulevard to Magnolia Boulevard. Fourteen years later the freeway was opened to Victory Boulevard, and two years after that the last stretch of the highway was opened to the Golden State Freeway. The state determined that the population center of California was located at Sherman Way and Fulton Avenue. As many people lived north of the intersection as south of it, and ditto east to west. North Hollywood was practically located in the

As an experiment to help pay off its debt load by boosting lunchtime business at the commissary, in 1964 the company quietly reinstated Carl Laemmle's trademark studio tours, which had been eliminated in the late 1920s with the introduction of sound equipment. Beginning as a modest Gray Line caravan, the tour traveled past the gothic house from *Psycho* (used

ABOVE: *Construction of the Hollywood Freeway near Vineland Avenue in 1957 caused so much debris in the immediate neighborhood that it was known as "Skunk Island." Note Cahuenga Pass in the center of this view, with the Universal City Studios in the background on the left. Courtesy, Universal City—North Hollywood Chamber of Commerce*

RIGHT: *When Universal City added an additional 140 acres to its property in 1950, it became the largest film studio in the world, with more than 420 acres of soundstages, back lots, and production facilities. Copyright © by Universal Pictures, a Division of Universal City Studios, Inc. Courtesy of MCA Publishing Rights, a Division of MCA Inc.*

in the film that was released by rival Paramount Studios but filmed at Universal City), around the set of *McHale's Navy* and through many of the historic western back-lot sets, where stuntmen performed a movie-style shoot-out for visitors. Admission was $2.50 for adults and $1.50 for children. In 1968 the studio tour gained its first national publicity on *The Today Show* and became one of the hottest tickets for tourists from around the world. Further enhancing Universal City's stature as a major tourist attraction, the 500-room, 20-story Sheraton-Universal Hotel opened early the next year.

On the Lankershim Boulevard flatlands below, the economic pressures created by the Valley Plaza and Laurel Plaza shopping-center behemoths and a migration of the affluent to the west Valley forced out of business many of the mom-and-pop specialty stores that had survived even the Depression. Replacing many of them was an influx of adult-entertainment businesses, including topless and bottomless striptease bars, pornography stores, and X-rated movie theaters. The area degenerated into a tenderloin and attracted to its late-night and early morning entertainment venues a nonresident clientele with no stake in the

Civic leaders and local businessmen gathered to celebrate the opening of the Hollywood Freeway to Magnolia Boulevard on July 16, 1962. Some prominent names included Tom Bane, Ray Nelson, Pete Fritz, Mario Negri, Fred Weddington, Jack Elliott, Dick Heppler, and Al Zoraster on the podium. Courtesy, Universal City—North Hollywood Chamber of Commerce

community's long-term health. Even the venerable Valley *Times* closed up shop.

Actress Beverly Garland, who has served as North Hollywood's mayor since 1975 and who operates the Beverly Garland Hotel on Vineland Avenue, remembers the depressed business climate in the years just before she opened her hotel in 1971. Garland said, "Lankershim Boulevard was really going downhill . . . It was really an area that nobody felt would really come back."

But resident home owners stuggled to maintain the wholesome atmosphere that had always typified the town.

Actor Tony Curtis takes a break from filming to show these armed forces troops a saber prop that was to be used in an upcoming Universal production in the 1950s. Courtesy, Universal City—North Hollywood Chamber of Commerce

North Hollywood business district and formed a "Committee for a New North Hollywood." With the support of the community's longtime corporate and individual activists—including Ted Rathbun, Martin Pollard, Bill McCann, Weddington Investment Company, Blanchard Lumber Company, Cutter Ford, and Security Pacific Bank—the committee raised $12,000 to fund a study of the area by the Economic Research Association (ERA).

In August 1969 the ERA report echoed the committee's goals and proposed the following: building a new regional shopping center; establishing a beautification program; linking the community more closely with Universal City; and creating a master plan for redevelopment. The rebuilding effort got off to a slow start, however, when a move to change the name of Lankershim Boulevard to Universal Boulevard failed.

The chamber of commerce, the Citizens' Action Committee, the Jaycees, the PTA, and other community groups fought to minimize the encroaching blight. They enlisted the help of the North Hollywood police, the Los Angeles County's Pornography and Obscenity Committee, the Los Angeles Police Commission, the Los Angeles City Council, and the California Alcoholic Beverage Control Commission.

In 1968 the chamber of commerce supported Guy Weddington McCreary's proposal to rebuild the

An additional temporary setback to the area's restoration came when the City of Los Angeles Community Redevelopment Agency (CRA) initially refused to assist any North Hollywood project. Participation by the CRA, which had such a tremendous impact on downtown Los Angeles and which had been instrumental in Glendale's development of its Galleria shopping center, was considered essential to the overall success of the project. The agency's

Summertime is enjoyed by this little one playing in the Valley Plaza Park sprinklers around 1960. Courtesy, Universal City—North Hollywood Chamber of Commerce

The overwhelming success of *Airport* started the studio on a run of monumental hits that included 1973's *The Sting* (which won the Oscar for Best Picture) and George Lucas' unexpectedly popular *American Graffiti;* 1974's theater-shaking Sensurround production of *Earthquake;* Steven Spielberg's first feature and box-office monster, *Jaws* (which earned $133 million for Universal in 1975); and 1978's Vietnam War drama, *Deer Hunter,* voted Best Picture.

In the summer of 1973 Universal opened its new 5,000-seat amphitheater with a production of *Jesus Christ Superstar* that was extended until cold weather forced the show's closing. After years of bitter dispute among rival organizations, the North Hollywood Chamber of Commerce was able to put a stop to the dismemberment of the town by the Sun Valley, Studio City, and Toluca Lake chambers when all four groups agreed to respect newly specified boundaries.

Dramatic progress on the North Hollywood community plan was marked on March 11, 1975, when the 13 members of the Los Angeles City Council unanimously approved it. Among its proposals were zoning limits to protect the single-family home, the rejuvenation of the central business district along Lankershim Boulevard, the construction of garden apartments, and a Metro Rail station. But virtually everyone agreed that without the involvement of the CRA, the plan would accomplish little.

The following year Joe Hurley, Weddington Investment Company, Blanchard Lumber, and other individuals and companies founded the nonprofit corporation Operation Gateway. Labeling its work "a renaissance by private enterprise in the public interest," Operation Gateway supported the redevelopment plan by presenting plans to potential developers, new businesses, and government agencies.

When 30,000 Fourth of July celebrants com-

power of eminent domain allowed it to combine small parcels of land and repackage them as properties large enough for profitable redevelopment.

As the population rose to 200,000 in 1971, the North Hollywood Jaycees dedicated in North Hollywood Park the Ernest Shelton sculpture of one of the community's most beloved residents: Amelia Earhart. (In 1981 the park's library was renamed for her.) Additional evidence of change on Lankershim Boulevard was seen when the landmark Rathbun's Department Store became the Naha's Department Store. Though it would remain in business until 1980, the loss of Rathbun's prestige dealt a severe blow to area merchants.

A little more than a year later, a 26-member Citizens Advisory Committee was formed by councilman Jim Potter in an effort to draw up a master community plan that might cause the CRA to reverse its earlier decision. With the completion of a draft plan 19 months later in October 1972, the city planning commission scheduled hearings. But Mayor Sam Yorty imposed severe restrictions on all such plans, and the proposal was put into limbo for almost the next two and a half years.

However, while North Hollywood continued to deteriorate, Universal City thrived. In 1970 the studio released *Airport,* a high-altitude nail-biter with a galaxy of stars. Nominated for 10 Academy Awards, it became Universal's biggest money-winner to date, pulling in $44.5 million, almost four times more than the studio's previous champ, *Spartacus.*

memorated the nation's bicentennial in North Hollywood Park, they were also witnessing the beginning of a new era in the rebirth of their town. The community had hit bottom and was bouncing back.

Early in 1977 the CRA formed an ad hoc Citizens Advisory Committee to verify that North Hollywood qualified for CRA participation. Less than a year later the slowly grinding wheels of government presented to the Los Angeles City Council a report on 740 acres of North Hollywood. With the strong support of councilman Joel Wachs, North Hollywood was on its way to becoming the first area of the Valley to have a CRA project. Shortly afterwards, elections for the 25-member Project Area Committee were held. The PAC continues to serve as a vital liaison between the CRA and the local community.

Revitalization was achieved through the CRA by rehabilitating existing residential, commercial, and industrial properties and promoting new uses for them; improving automobile- and pedestrian-traffic flow; con-

structing new utilities, parks, benches, signs, and public buildings; and, "reparceling" small pieces of land into larger ones.

In 1979 the Los Angeles City Council approved a $96-million, 740-acre CRA redevelopment plan for North Hollywood. Immediate improvements were the Hewlett-Packard regional sales headquarters building at the southwest corner of Lankershim and Magnolia boulevards and the Magnolia Towers, senior-citizen housing at the northwest corner of Magnolia Boulevard and Vineland Avenue.

During the early 1980s Universal City blossomed into one of the world's greatest attractions. In 1982 the amphitheater was redesigned and enclosed to become one of Los Angeles' most comfortable theaters. The Registry Hotel (now The Universal City Hilton and Towers) joined the Sheraton-Universal in providing first-class accommodations. Steven Spielberg's sentimental E.T.—The Extra-Terrestrial lured audiences in droves and became the number-one success in the history of motion pictures, racking up $700 million in revenues (with videocassette sales adding more millions in the late 1980s).

Three years later, another Universal science-fiction film hit the box-office jackpot when TV star Michael J. Fox's Back to the Future took in more than $100 million and provided the prototype for two sequels. That year Universal's Out of Africa won the Academy Award for Best Picture.

The studio tour was expanded to become a seven-hour extravaganza featuring several attractions based on all-time movie hits, including Jaws,

Earthquake—The Big One, Conan the Barbarian, Star Trek, King Kong, and *Back to the Future.* Entertaining up to 40,000 guests a day—as many as the first tour drew in a year—the Universal Studios Hollywood theme park became the fourth most popular tourist attraction in the United States, with 5 million visitors annually.

In 1984 MCA and Texaco jointly participated in the construction of the towering 10 Universal City Plaza Building. At 36 stories, it became the tallest building in the San Fernando Valley. Universal's success at box offices around the world swelled the studio's

facilities and work force. Up to 10,000 filmmakers, actors, technicians, and associated support staff filled the lot's 34 soundstages every day.

In 1985 Universal City joined the North Hollywood Chamber of Commerce to more effectively represent the interests of both communities. An 18-screen Cineplex Odeon cinema opened in Universal City in July 1987 and became the largest such facility in the country. The "Streets of the World" section re-created avenues in London and Paris. With a full range of Hollywood-themed attractions, Universal City realized its goal of becoming "The Entertain-

ment Capital of the World."

As part of the CRA's North Hollywood project, in the early 1980s, Kensley Group partner Ken Adkins approached the Academy of Television Arts and Sciences about lending its name to a billion-dollar, 22-acre project he envisioned for Lankershim Boulevard's traditional commercial core. The Television Academy agreed to participate, and plans were drawn up for the $40-million Phase One of the Academy Project.

The six phases for the project, to be completed in about 10 years, feature over 1.5 million square feet of office space, almost 200,000 square feet of prime retail and restaurant space, a 218-room hotel, 400 residential units, as well as the Television Academy's headquarters, Hall of Fame Plaza (with its gleaming 18-foot statue of Emmy), and the 600-seat, state-of-the-art Academy Theater.

In 1987 the Universal City—North Hollywood Chamber of Commerce founded a charitable foundation, which organized its first annual Charity Starscene festival. A three-day event held in North Hollywood Park during the third weekend in August, Starscene has become the Valley's premier charity event and a highpoint in the North Hollywood calendar of activities. This colorful fair, attended by local entertainment and sports celebrities as well as thousands of visitors, contributes all of its proceeds to various charities, particularly those which focus their activities on children's programs.

During North Hollywood's centennial year in 1988, ground was broken for Phase One of the Academy Project, and its opening in August 1990 guaranteed North Hollywood's rejuvenation. Three additional "Designs for Development" projects are under CRA consideration elsewhere in North Hollywood. If approved, they would provide ultramodern shopping facilities, office space, and housing.

On election night, November 6, 1990, Santa Ana winds fanned a spectacular fire that lit up the sky and could have served as footage for a Universal disaster film as it destroyed about 20 percent of the historic back lot. The sets that were incinerated included those seen in *To Kill a Mockingbird, The Sting, Back to the Future,* and *Dick Tracy.* Also reduced to cinders were New York Street, Georgetown Avenue, Warehouse Street, and Brownstone Street. The damage was estimated at $25 million, with reconstruction scheduled to take six months.

Fortunately, the company's film vault was saved, and no significant damage was suffered by any of the major attractions on the studio tour, which re-

sumed the next day and took curious sightseers past the still-smoldering ruins. Also during Universal City's 75th anniversary, MCA announced the sale of the company to Japan's largest electronics company, Matsushita Electric Industrial Company (whose brand names include Panasonic). The purchase price was estimated at about $6.59 billion, or about $71 per share. With 17,000 employees—including thousands in Universal Studios Florida, which opened earlier in the year—earning $192 million in profits in 1990 on revenues of $3.4 billion, the deal represented the largest sale of an American company to a Japanese firm to date.

The next decade holds a myriad of promises for Universal City and North Hollywood, including a Metro Rail station adjacent to Campo de Cahuenga and a second station several miles north, near the Academy Project. Also planned are a new police station and courthouse, and with the Laurel Plaza expansion, the Lankershim Boulevard revitalization-and-beautification project, the prestigious new Laurel Hall Preparatory School, and Universal's multimillion-

The old mission room seems dark and gloomy. It is midnight while I write; and the flickering candle gives but a sombre light.

Voices in the air are telling me what this Valley will become: Bright lights, dancing, music, the busy hum of a city vast and large, streets that would shame the Paris of today and cause the great Strand in London to feel poor and pitiful to traverse our Valley.

Where the coyote roamed and the antelope came to drink there are buildings that vie in elegance with the perfect proportions of the Pantheon of Rome. I shall not be here to see it, nor will you; but the mountains will watch it, and the sun will shine upon it, and the breezes from the sea will bring refreshing coolness.

And I do believe and I do think that One who loves this place—and all of you, my neighbors as much as I—will look down upon it with pride and thoughtfulness.

Then advance in prosperity, my much beloved Valley. Let the teachings of the past give to the youths and maidens of the future the wisdom of experience as all must learn!! Advance! My much beloved Valley.

Through the brazen vales of time, let this be a place of happiness and prosperity and the names of the people that have helped to make you be as household names.

dollar CityWalk project, the area's continued vitality seems assured.

Now, from the top-floor restaurant of the Sheraton-Universal Hotel, the lights burning in the homes on the North Hollywood hills and on the floor of the Valley below evoke memories of the Indian campfires that dotted the area 250 years ago. At the foot of the hotel, Campo de Cahuenga serves as a living reminder of the rancho era of Andrés Pico, who, in the year before he died, prophesized in the San Fernando Mission's Convento building:

Partners in Progress

About a century before songwriter Gordon Jenkins wrote his famous hit song, "I'm Gonna Make the San Fernando Valley My Home," U.S. Army lieutenant colonel John C. Frémont met with Mexican general Andrés Pico at the Campo de Cahuenga, now a historical monument in North Hollywood. The year was 1847, and the purpose of the meeting was to sign a treaty ending the Mexican-American War.

Less than 25 years later, two men whose names would be forever after linked with the history of the San Fernando Valley, Isaac Lankershim and Isaac Newton Van Nuys, purchased the entire southern half of the Valley, nearly 60,000 acres, and began growing wheat. The cost of the land was $115,000, far less than the average price of one home in the area today.

Lankershim died in 1882, and in 1887 the Lankershim Land Ranch and Water Company purchased 12,000 acres from his estate. W.H. Andrews was hired as superintendent, the land was cleared, and 50,000 peach and apricot trees were planted. The first business establishments, a hotel and a general store, opened the following year. Originally called Toluca, meaning "fertile valley," the area was then known as Toluca/Lankershim.

In 1890 Wilson C. Weddington brought his wife and two sons, Guy and Fred, from Iowa to visit his sister Mollie, who had married W.H. Andrews. The Weddingtons liked what they saw and decided to relocate permanently in Southern California. With about 10 other families, they established the town of Lankershim which, under their leadership, would grow and flourish.

In 1893 Wilson Weddington became the area's first postmaster, and two years later his sons purchased the general store, which became known as Weddington Brothers. In 1904 Guy Weddington became president of Bonner Fruit Company, the largest employer in the area.

The town's first newspaper appeared in 1909, and one year later the Bank of Lankershim was formed, as the community's population reached the 500 mark. The boom continued, fueled by the arrival of the famous Big Red streetcars in 1911. In 1912 Bavarian immigrant Carl Laemmle acquired 230 acres and founded the Universal Film Manufacturing Company, forerunner of the world-famous Universal Studios.

Today Universal City is home not only to the fourth-largest theme park in the United States, the Universal Studios Tour, but is also home to 10 Universal City Plaza, the tallest building in the San Fernando Valley. Its 36 stories include 865,000 square feet of office space and a seven-level parking structure.

In 1923 the town of Lankershim was officially annexed to the city of Los Angeles, and in 1927 the name was changed to North Hollywood.

The Universal City—North Hollywood area today is one of the most dynamic communities in Southern California. It is home to thousands of widely diversified businesses, large and small, including shopping, entertainment, fine dining, tourist attractions, historic landmarks, manufacturers, major corporate offices, and virtually every other type of business and profession.

The stories of some of these organizations, which have chosen to participate in this literary project, are told on the following pages.

The Lankershim residents who participated in this May 1900 Sunday School picnic enjoyed a glorious day at the old Ostrich Farm, an area that is now part of Griffith Park. Courtesy, Weddington Family Collection

Universal City-North Hollywood Chamber of Commerce

The town of Lankershim, as North Hollywood was once called, was mostly a farm community when the Lankershim Chamber of Commerce was formed. The year was 1914, and Jim Wilson was named the first president. The population was about 1,500 and there was only a handful of businesses.

Almost from inception, the chamber of commerce was a focal point of community leadership, and for more than three-quarters of a century has played a major role in virtually every significant event in the development of North Hollywood. In 1923 it was active in the campaign to annex Lankershim to the City of Los Angeles, which was approved in a closely contested election.

In 1927 the chamber led a successful drive to change the community's name to North Hollywood and played a major role in the passage of a $378,000 bond issue, used to purchase the 99-acre property that became North Hollywood Park. Originally called North Hollywood Municipal Playground, it was dedicated in 1930. One acre of the property was allocated for a library, completed in 1929. Formerly the North Hollywood East Valley Library, it was renamed the Amelia Earhart Branch Library in 1981, in honor of the community's most famous citizen.

During the Depression the chamber was headquarters for unemployment relief in the Valley, and when World War II broke out it became Civil Defense Headquarters. With the dawn of the postwar era the chamber reorganized, as North Hollywood (then a community of 100,000) was enjoying unprecedented growth.

In 1951 the chamber led what proved to be an unsuccessful campaign to preserve the famous Pacific Electric Red Cars, which had served the area since 1911. But as new freeways were built, the automobile be-

Throughout the years the chamber of commerce has been a focal point of area leadership.

came king and the Red Cars took their last ride.

By the 1950s the chamber's membership exceeded 800 businesses. In 1957 it set up a new Industrial Committee, which hosted a conference attended by more than 500 industrial companies. During the 1960s the chamber formed a More Modern Downtown North Hollywood Committee and set up a Women's Division, which remained in place until 1983.

In 1976 the chamber formed Operation Gateway to push for the formation of a Community Redevelopment Agency, paving the way for the San Fernando Valley's first CRA project, in North Hollywood. Some

$200 million to date has been invested in redevelopment, with the figure expected to reach $500 million to one billion dollars by the turn of the century. At the heart of the redevelopment is the Academy Project on Lankershim Boulevard, the new home of the Academy of Television Arts and Sciences.

In 1987 the chamber formed the Universal City-North Hollywood Chamber Charitable Foundation, which produced the largest annual charity festival in the San Fernando Valley, the three-day Charity Star Scene. The foundation has expanded its activities to include a golf tournament, movie premieres, and a 5-kilometer run, as well as special activities for retarded and underprivileged children. The resources of the foundation benefit the surrounding community, the Valley, and selected charities.

One of the chamber's enduring traditions has been the selection of an honorary mayor of North Hollywood. The first one, back in 1938, was actress Glenda Farrell, who was followed by such luminaries as Gene Autry, Gordon Jenkins (who wrote the famous song, "I'm Gonna Make the San Fernando Valley My Home"), Ann Blyth, Yvonne DeCarlo, Andy Griffith, and Beverly Garland, who has served in that post since 1973.

Today the Universal City-North Hollywood Chamber of Commerce is an organization of dedicated business, industrial, and professional community members, working together to create the best possible climate for increased business, civic, and industrial prosperity for all and to improve the quality of life for the entire community.

Weddington Investment

For more than a century, there hardly seems to have been one significant event in North Hollywood that has not involved a member of the Weddington family—truly the first family of North Hollywood.

Wilson Weddington was born in Indiana in 1847. In 1866 he moved to Iowa, where he married Mary Ann Rutledge and became a farmer, sheriff, and father of two sons, Guy and Fred. Wilson Weddington might have remained an Iowan had it not been for a visit to his sister, Molie, who moved to California in 1886 with her husband, W.H. Andrews, superintendent for the Lankershim Ranch Land and Water Company. After one look at Toluca, Weddington bought property there and settled his family in what was to become the townsite of North Hollywood.

In 1893 President Grover Cleveland appointed Weddington postmaster of Toluca/Lankershim. One year later Weddington acquired the Wilcox store; it soon became the primary store and post office for the area. Around 1907 Guy Weddington bought Bonner Fruit Company, and Guy became president of that major local employer that canned tons of fruit for the eastern market.

In 1910 the Weddingtons established the Bank of Lankershim and incorporated Weddington Investment Company, with Wilson Weddington as president. In 1911 he drove in the gold spike that signaled the arrival of the famed Red Car line in the San Fernando Valley. With his sons he helped form the Lankershim Chamber of Commerce in 1914.

Guy Weddington, vice president of Weddington Investment, became president of the company after his father's death in 1923. He served over the years as director of Hollywood National Bank, Bank of Lankershim, Lankershim Development Company, and North Hollywood Savings and Loan, and served as president of North Hollywood Chamber of Commerce from 1927 to 1929. Guy was a member of Lankershim Kiwanis, a Mason, and was a leader in the name changing of Lankershim to North Hollywood and the purchase of North Hollywood Park in 1927. In the 1930s he dedicated the North Hollywood Post Office site and supported the opening of Cahuenga Pass.

Guy Weddington died in 1941 and was succeeded as president of Weddington Investment by his brother, Fred. Fred was the first constable of Lankershim in 1903. He graduated from Woodbury Business College and helped form the Lankershim Development Company. In 1910 Fred became president of the Bank of Lankershim, and in 1927 a charter member of the North Hollywood Rotary and a Mason. He served as a vice president of North Hollywood's Security Pacific bank until his retirement in 1949. Fred dedicated North and South Weddington Parks in 1960. He died in 1967, survived by his daughter, Betty Becker, and his four grandsons: Ernie, Jr., Barry, Randy, and Bruce.

Guy's son, Milo

Pioneer Wilson C. Weddington—soldier, sheriff, postmaster, farmer, and businessman—and his two sons played a dominant role in the early development of what today is North Hollywood.

Weddington, succeeded his uncle Fred as president of Weddington Investment, a position Milo held until his death in 1984. He had also been a banker, retiring from Security Pacific Bank as a vice president after a 34-year career. He left two sons, Page and William.

Following Milo's death, his nephew Guy Weddington McCreary became president. Guy continues the family tradition of community service, including serving as president of the Jaycees, involvement in the Amelia Earhart Statue Project, a member of the Kiwanis, as chairman of the citizen advisory committee for a community plan, as president of the North Hollywood Chamber of Commerce in 1980, as a member of the CRA Project Area Committee for redevelopment of North Hollywood, and as a nominee for the Fernando Award in 1989. Guy has one son, Jonathan Davis.

In 1987 Weddington Investment became a family partnership that invests in and manages properties. Fittingly its offices are located on Weddington Street. The 1941 book *Our Town* by Lincoln Hart describes early San Fernando Valley pioneers as people of faith and vision. This definition is easily applied to the Weddington family who has served the community with distinction for four generations.

This photo, taken in 1908, shows a horse and buggy and a horseless carriage parked in front of the store managed by Guy and Fred Weddington since 1894. The building also housed the post office run by their father, Wilson Weddington, the area's first postmaster.

Brite Lite Neon Corporation

To describe Brite Lite Neon Corporation as a family business is an understatement. Founded in 1952 by James Joseph Mastopietro, the company now employs 11 family members—about one-third of the entire staff.

Mastopietro moved to the San Fernando Valley from Milwaukee, Wisconsin, where he had been in the sign business. He opened Brite Lite in a small facility on Burbank Boulevard in North Hollywood, between Vineland and Cahuenga. His brother-in-law, Enrico "Ric" Cincis, soon followed him from Milwaukee to help get the business launched. Both men are still involved with the firm, the former as president and the latter as vice president.

Over the years the business and the family kept growing; today four Mastopietro sons and one daughter are on board, along with three Cincis sons and one daughter. The company has long since left that first plant, moving several times to larger and larger quarters. In 1983 it purchased its present 25,000-square-foot facility at 5536 Satsuma Avenue. The original staff of four has grown to more than 30 employees.

As its name indicates, the company's primary products are neon signs, and its customers include many major retailers and financial institutions. Brite Lite also does work for movie and television studios, with its products used on several popular game shows. Sign sizes range from as small as two square feet up to 300 square feet or more. One sign measured 48 by 25 feet, and a recent studio set sign included letters that are more than nine feet high and two feet wide.

The company does both fabrication and installation. Signs are made of sheet metal, with plastic faces and neon lights. Glass tubes of varying lengths are purchased and then shaped as needed. Sales are primarily in Southern and Northern California, although Brite Lite does ship nationwide to certain customers.

The sign business has become far more elaborate than it was when Brite Lite was founded. Signage is now incorporated in new construction right from the start. The company gets involved during the architectural phase, with signs designed right along with the building. Signs are no longer simply hung on a structure after its completion. Some become an integral part of a structure, as was the case with the arches at the entrances to the Topanga Plaza. Brite Lite also does a lot of the ambient interior lighting incorporated in new projects.

Since launching their business in North Hollywood, company officials have been actively involved in the community. Longtime members of the Universal City-North Hollywood Chamber of Commerce, they also support other organizations, including the American Cancer Society, the March of Dimes, and Father Flanagan's Boys Home. For many years Jim Mastopietro has also participated in the Burbank Art Association. He is an accomplished artist, and the walls of his company's offices are lined with his paintings, several of which have won awards.

It seems an appropriate hobby for the founder of a company whose products require as much art as technology. Not confined to a museum, the masterpieces of Brite Lite Neon Corporation can be seen everywhere, atop major department stores and financial institutions, in local shops and restaurants, and in movie theaters and on television screens.

Mooney & Murphy

F. Bentley Mooney, Jr., senior member of the North Hollywood law firm of Mooney & Murphy, began practicing with a local firm in 1972 at the age of 36. He later became a partner in that firm and left to establish his own in 1981. In 1989 his firm became known as Mooney & Murphy. Before entering the legal profession, Mooney, a California native, enjoyed a successful 14-year career in life insurance sales and management, beginning in 1958. He earned the CLU (Chartered Life Underwriter) designation in 1963 and later served as a general agent for John Hancock Life and still later as superintendent of agencies for Southland Life.

Mooney & Murphy specializes in business law and litigation, estate planning, probate, and asset protection planning. Its client base is composed primarily of 200 small- to medium-size business firms.

F. Bentley Mooney, Jr.

Slightly more than half of the practice involves litigation, led and managed by Michael C. Murphy.

One of the firm's more innovative services, introduced in 1985, is its telephone retainer program. For an annual fee of $150, clients receive unlimited business and personal legal advice via telephone, encouraging them to call while potential problems are still in their early stages. Clients also receive without charge the firm's custom newsletter, covering issues of importance and concern to business owners.

In addition to practicing law, Mooney has written several books. They include a trilogy published in 1986: *Handcuff the Tax Man, Going Bare,* and *The Artful Use of Offshore Tax Havens.* Two other books of his were published in 1988: *When Health Is Lost: Providing for the Costs of Long-Term Nursing Care* deals with planning for Medi-Cal eligibility; *Cluster! A Flexible Approach to the Cluster Agency Maze* is a monograph addressed to independent insurance agencies.

Murphy, a native of Los Angeles, entered practice in 1981 and joined Mooney in 1983. In addition to variously conducting or supervising the firm's litigation activities, he serves as general counsel for the Universal City/North

Michael C. Murphy

Hollywood Chamber of Commerce and the Chemical Abuse Prevention Foundation. Both men give liberally of their time to worthwhile civic and charitable organizations.

F. Bentley Mooney, Jr., is a past president of the Kiwanis Club of North Hollywood and held or holds leadership posts with the Christian Business Men's Committee, the Universal City/North Hollywood Chamber of Commerce, the First Baptist Church at La Crescenta, and several professional groups at the local, county, and state levels. In addition to the activities already mentioned, Michael C. Murphy is a member and former secretary of the North Hollywood Rotary Club and serves on the board of directors of St. Elizabeth's Convalescent Hospital. Both men are members of the American Bar Association, the State Bar of California, and the Los Angeles County Bar Association.

VDA Property Company

There is little in the background of Charles K. "Chuck" and Thomas R. "Tom" Von Der Ahe to indicate career paths in real estate development and management. In fact, based on heredity and early training, the Von Der Ahe brothers could easily be in the retail grocery business. And that is exactly where they were for many years before forming VDA Property Company.

One of California's major food chains, Von's Grocery Co., was founded by members of the Von Der Ahe family in the 1930s. Wilfred and Ted Von Der Ahe, father and uncle, respectively, of Chuck and Tom, founded the chain. For them, it was doing what comes naturally. Wilfred and Ted's father, Charles Von Der Ahe, had started a retail grocery business, also called Von's, back in 1906 which grew to a chain of 100 stores. He sold the company just prior to the Great Depression, but his sons, who had grown up in the business, decided to start out on their own a few years later.

Chuck and Tom Von Der Ahe also grew up in the grocery business. Before finishing elementary school, they had begun working in the family markets after school and during summer vacations. They did a variety of jobs, including working as box boys, checkers, stock clerks, and receiving clerks, throughout their high school and college years. After the brothers graduated from Loyola University—Chuck in 1959 and Tom in 1963—they joined Von's full time, with increasing responsibilities.

Some of those responsibilities involved store planning, design, construction, and layout, giving the brothers their first experience in what would later become their chosen profession. As the 1960s drew to a close, Chuck was serving as director of store operations and Tom as assistant sales manager.

But the entrepreneurial in-

(From left) Wilfred Von Der Ahe, Sr., Tom Von Der Ahe, and Charles Von Der Ahe.

stincts of their grandfather, father, and uncle were very much present, and Tom and Chuck spent many hours talking about launching their own business. For awhile, they seriously considered opening their own grocery store but decided retailing was no longer for them.

In 1972 they left Von's to found VDA Property Company. They opened a small office at 4040 Vineland in North Hollywood and hired a secretary. Their first venture was the purchase of the land and the construction of the eight-story office building that now stands at 4605 Lankershim Boulevard. VDA Property was the first tenant, moving into the 117,000-square-foot building in January 1974. It is still there, as both owner and manager of what has become a highly desirable and fully occupied building.

VDA has also developed several other projects in Southern California, including two racquetball and tennis facilities: the Racquet Centre of South Pasadena and the Racquet Centre of Universal City. The firm also constructed a Northridge bank

headquarters project consisting of a 28,000-square-foot structure and two 9,000-square-foot restaurants. Other projects include a 17,000-square-foot office building in North Hollywood called Vineland Garden and two apartment projects in Glendale containing 35 and 33 units, respectively.

VDA Property Company is also in the property management business and operates all of the above-listed facilities and several others, including three bank buildings in the Inland Empire, a shopping center/office complex in Downey, and four multi-unit apartment buildings in Torrance. The firm also has an ownership interest in all of its projects, through a subsidiary, VDA Property, Inc., of which Tom and Chuck Von Der Ahe are the sole stockholders. The corporation is the general partner on all VDA projects.

The Von Der Ahe brothers were born and raised within three miles of their headquarters and have deep roots in North Hollywood. Both par-

VDA Property Company's first venture was the purchase of land and the construction of an eight-story office building at 4605 Lankershim Boulevard.

ticipate actively in a variety of community organizations. Chuck is a past chairman of the board of regents of Loyola Marymount University and has served as a board member of the North Hollywood Chamber of Commerce, Notre Dame High School, St. Joseph Medical Foundation, and the Notre Dame University Club of Los Angeles.

Tom Von Der Ahe is a past vice chairman and has served on the board of directors of Campbell Hall School and as president of its Parent/ Teachers Council. He is a member of the chambers of commerce in North Hollywood and Toluca Lake as well as the Jonathon Club of Los Angeles and the Lake Arrowhead Yacht Club.

The brothers are avid golfers and have held leadership posts at Lakeside Country Club in North Hollywood. Tom is a past president, and Chuck served as secretary of the board of directors. They also enjoy tennis, paddle tennis, and racquetball.

VDA Property Company now employs a staff of 70 people to manage its growing and widespread operations. There is one office set aside for another Von Der Ahe, who reports for work daily. He is Chuck and Tom's father, Wilfred, who joined his sons after retiring from Von's Grocery Company.

The senior Von Der Ahe's heart is still in the grocery business, and he regularly urges his sons to set their sights back in that direction. Perhaps one day some of his grandchildren will go to work for the giant retail grocery company he helped found.

Both Chuck and Tom have large families. Tom and his wife, Celeste, are the parents of six children, while Chuck and his wife, Eleanor, have eight children between them. To date, none work for VDA Property Company but, with 14 in all, that is likely to change.

MCA Inc.

MCA Inc. is the parent company of Universal Studios, the oldest and largest existing motion picture studio in Hollywood.

Carl Laemmle, an immigrant from Bavaria, founded the Universal Film Manufacturing Co. on June 8, 1912. Nearly three years later Laemmle opened the gates of a 230-acre ranch he had purchased for $165,000, and Universal City became the first self-contained, unincorporated community dedicated to making movies.

Today the vast film colony has become a thriving industrial giant. The studio that once had 400 people on its payroll now employs 10,000 filmmakers, actors, technicians, and service personnel during peak production times.

On its expanded 420 acres are 34 sound stages; a 15-story office building; a 200,000-square-foot office complex; twin Technicolor Inc. motion picture film laboratories; the 20-story, 450-room Sheraton-Universal Hotel and the 450-room Universal City Hilton and Towers; and, as part of its tremendous back lot, waterfalls, lakes, and standing outdoor sets that range from European streets and frontier towns of the Old West to American cities and suburbs.

The famous Psycho *house has become something of a landmark on the Universal backlot.*

The Universal Studios Tour, the third largest theme park in the United States, gives visitors a behind-the-scenes glimpse at the way movies are made.

Other facilities on the site, the largest contiguous property held by a single owner in Los Angeles County, include the 6,251-seat Universal Amphitheatre; a 75,000-square-foot office complex; the Alfred Hitchcock Theatre; several restaurants; a 180,000-square-foot technical building; a two-story entertainment center, housing 18 wide-screen motion picture theaters; 10 Universal City Plaza, a 36-story, 750,000-square-foot office tower; and the third-largest theme park in the United States, the famous Universal Studios Tour, which attracts millions of visitors annually.

Universal's role in filmmaking spans every decade of the twentieth century. Founder Carl Laemmle, who died in 1936 at the age of 72, made his first motion picture in 1909—the one-reel *Hiawatha*. In 1911 Universal made its initial West Coast venture, buying Nestor Studios in Hollywood. Three years later, Laemmle purchased the 230-acre Taylor Estate in Lankershim Township on the north side of the Hollywood Hills, just across the road from the site where, in 1846, Mexican General Andres Pico and U.S. Colonel John Fremont signed the treaty of Cahuenga, ceding the California territory to the United States.

The first year of operation at the new studio saw 250 films produced. The first film completed was *Damon and Pythias*, in which Universal City's first mayor, Herbert Rawlinson, played Pythias. Thousands of films have followed, including nine of the 30 most commercially successful movies of all time.

Shortly after MCA purchased Universal in 1959, the company greatly increased its emphasis on television. A year earlier, MCA had acquired about 700 pre-1948 films owned by Paramount; the subsequent screenings of those films on television generated millions of dollars in revenue for the company. Universal Television has been a pioneer in many other ways as well, with syndicating reruns of TV shows; producing the first world premiere made-for-television film; and Operation Prime Time. Over the years the company has produced a wide range of popular, diverse, and award-winning programs and miniseries.

The Motion Picture Group and the Television Group are just two of the many enterprises of MCA Inc., which is involved in virtually every phase of the entertainment industry. Also operating under the parent company umbrella are the Music Entertainment Group; the Recreation Group; the Consumer Products Group; the Home Entertainment Group; MCA Development Company; MCA Broadcasting; and MCA Enterprises. From its home base in Universal City, the impact of MCA Inc. is felt around the world.

Frazier Aviation

Like many another business success stories, Frazier Aviation began in humble surroundings—the garage and yard of the home of founder Robert L. Frazier, Jr. Frazier, a Kansas native and University of Kansas graduate, came to California in 1934 to work for McDonnell Douglas Corporation. He left the company after 18 years, and with a $500 investment formed his own firm, primarily as a broker/dealer and supplier of aviation parts to his former employer and to the U.S. government.

A year later, in 1953, he moved into an 800-square-foot office in Hollywood. In 1956 his growing company relocated to a 4,000-square-foot building, and in 1964 to a 10,000-square-foot facility at its current location on Hartland Street in North Hollywood, which has since been expanded to 30,000 square feet.

In 1958, shortly after the business was incorporated, Frazier's wife, Lee, joined the company. She and her husband met at McDonnell Douglas where, for 10 years, she served as assistant to the vice president of manufacturing and expediting. During the company's early years, she handled the books while her husband was responsible for sales. Following his untimely death in 1976, she became president and chairman of the board, posts she still holds.

In 1960 another McDonnell Douglas veteran, Charles Ricard, joined the company and today serves as chief executive officer. In 1971 Bob and Lee's son, Robert III, was added to the team. A law student at the time his father became ill, he switched to business, earning his MBA degree from Loyola. Today he is director of manufacturing and costing.

In the early 1960s the company branched into sheet metal fabrication, and in 1963 into machining of custom aviation parts. It has enjoyed substantial growth over the years, maturing into a full-service sub-

ABOVE: Today (from left) Robert L. Frazier III is Frazier Aviation's director of manufacturing and costing, Lee P. Frazier serves as president and chairman of the board, and Charles E. Ricard is the company's chief executive officer.

LEFT: Robert L. Frazier, Jr.

contractor with the capability of design, manufacture, service, and sales of aerospace parts for both nonproduction and production aircraft, commercial as well as military. Over the years Frazier has supplied its customers with more than 60,000 different parts, a tribute to its versatility.

The company's largest customer is McDonnell Douglas, with which it has worked for more than 30 years. About 30 percent of annual revenues are from that source, another 30 percent from the U.S. Air Force, and the balance from a broad mix of commercial and military production. Frazier also supplies parts to foreign countries for nonproduction aircraft.

— Frazier Aviation, largely because

of the vision of its founder, has remained in the forefront of every phase of its operation. Its manufacturing equipment includes state-of-the-art computerized machinery. The company, which now has a staff of about 50 people, was one of the first in California to offer an Employee Stock Ownership Plan (ESOP). Today about 25 percent of the stock is owned by employees, with the Frazier family holding about 52 percent.

The vision and the legacy of Robert L. Frazier, Jr., are perhaps best summed up in these words, which he wrote not long before his death: "Man has come a long way, from universal clay to gathering moon dust, and for every accolade of achievement there is another more boundless, hidden in the shadow of the next horizon, waiting patiently for discovery in the stillness of infinity. For man has just begun his long journey, to soar the wind—spaceward."

Hurley, Grassini & Wrinkle

In 1950 Joseph G. Hurley decided to come to Southern California and sink his roots in North Hollywood. The Pennsylvania-born attorney, a graduate of the Catholic University of America in Washington, D.C., worked as an insurance adjuster while studying for the bar and was admitted to practice in California in 1953.

Hurley joined a small law firm with offices at 11313 Weddington Street in North Hollywood; he bought out the practice in 1955. With a staff of two secretaries, he specialized in personal injury cases, product liability, and insurance litigation. Today his much larger firm, still located at the same address, represents plaintiffs exclusively in those fields, with all cases handled on a contingency basis.

In 1972 Hurley joined forces with another transplanted Easterner, Lawrence P. Grassini, to form the partnership of Hurley & Grassini. Born and raised on New York's Long Island, Grassini received his bachelor's degree from St. Bonaventure University in Olean, New York, and his law degree from his partner's alma mater, Catholic University in Washington, D.C. Admitted to the California Bar in 1971, he served as a clerk to a federal judge before joining Hurley.

In 1976 Roland Wrinkle joined the firm, which was then incorporated as Hurley, Grassini & Wrinkle. Born and raised in North Hollywood, he received his undergraduate degree from California State University at Los Angeles and his law degree from the University of California at Los Angeles. During law school he worked for the firm, the only one with which he has ever been affiliated.

The firm, which now has several associates and support personnel, has enjoyed outstanding success in its specialized fields of practice and is rated among the top five plaintiff firms in California. Hurley modestly credits much of its success to his two younger partners, whom he describes as "two of the brightest lawyers in the country."

RIGHT: (From left) partners Joseph G. Hurley, Ronald Wrinkle, and Lawrence P. Grassini. Photo by Joe La Russo

BELOW: Pat Murphy, an associate with the firm, greets a client. Photo by Joe La Russo

Teamwork has been another important contributing factor, says Hurley. "We've been together for a long time, which is unusual in this field," he says. Several people are involved with each client and every case is reviewed and critiqued by the senior members of the firm.

In winning many multimillion-dollar cases, Hurley, Grassini & Wrinkle has established the best record of any plaintiff firm in the area. A $27.5-million verdict in favor of a client in a product liability case is the largest single personal-injury judgment paid in the history of the United States. The firm also represented well-known ventriloquist Paul Winchell in his 10-year fight against Metrome-dia, in which a jury awarded Winchell $17.8 million. In another case, a record $26-million out-of-court settlement was negotiated by the firm.

Joe Hurley, Larry Grassini, and Roland Wrinkle have all contributed extensively to professional and community activities. Hurley served for two terms as president of the Universal City/North Hollywood Chamber of Commerce and is a former vice president of the State Bar of California. He has served as president of the Burbank Bar Association, as a member of the board of trustees of the Los Angeles County Bar, and on the Judicial Council of the State of California. He is also a member of the Bar Association of the District of Columbia.

For more than a dozen years, Hurley has served as president of the Los Angeles-based Ralph M. Parsons Foundation, which has provided millions of dollars of support to many organizations in education, social impact, and civic, cultural, health, and special projects. He is also on the board of governors of the Music

ABOVE: *Lawrence Grassini does some research in the office library. Photo by Joe La Russo*

LEFT: *Joseph Hurley (standing) speaks with four associate attorneys. Photo by Joe La Russo*

Center of Los Angeles.

In 1988 Grassini served as president of the Los Angeles Trial Lawyers Association and is a former trustee of the Los Angeles County Bar Association. He also serves on the board of governors of the California Trial Lawyers Association. Grassini has appeared as a panelist and lecturer before numerous conventions and trial lawyer associations and has won many awards for his legal work.

In 1983, 1985, and 1986 he was chosen by Verdictum Juris (compilers of jury verdicts) as the Plaintiff Trial Lawyer of the Year, and is the only person to ever receive that award more than once. He was also selected by the Los Angeles Trial Lawyers Association as the Trial Lawyer of the Year in 1983. When named again in 1986,

he became the first person to be so honored twice.

Wrinkle is a past president of the Burbank Bar Association and serves on the board of governors of the Los Angeles Trial Lawyers Association. For many years he has been appellate editor of the latter association's journal, *The Advocate*. His monthly column, called "After The Dust Settles," keeps trial lawyers abreast of the latest developments in their field.

To help redevelop North Hollywood, Joe Hurley founded Operation Gateway. With contributions from Fred Massimini, the Weddington Investment Co., North Hollywood Federal Savings and Loan (now Coast Savings), and the Von Der Ahe family, Operation Gateway became the spearhead of what is the Community Redevelopment Project changing the face of North Hollywood today.

He has never wavered from that decision he made to settle in North Hollywood. "If I had it to do all over again," Hurley says, "I would not change a thing."

Kensley Group

It was 1980 when Kenneth H. Adkins first saw "the chance to make a significant impact on the community of North Hollywood." The San Fernando Valley native, whose father had lived in North Hollywood prior to World War II, had recently embarked on a career in real estate development after 12 years in the investment banking industry.

The Kensley Group, of which he is a co-founder, was launched in 1980 in Beverly Hills. As co-chairman of that group of companies and partnerships, he was part of a team that conceived a major redevelopment plan for North Hollywood, the location of his home. Unwilling to embark on a project of such great magnitude without significant community support, he talked with virtually all the leaders of North Hollywood.

The support he sought was immediately forthcoming, and he began meeting with the Los Angeles Community Redevelopment Agency to plan what would evolve into a 20-year-long project to change the face of North Hollywood's famous Lankershim Boulevard. Once the main route to Northern California, Lankershim in 1980 was little more than the main street of a typical small town U.S.A.

Adkins decided that a theme on which his project could focus was essential and that focus became the entertainment industry, specifically television. He met with the president of the Academy of Television Arts and Sciences to suggest North Hollywood as the site for its first permanent home. Once housed in North Hollywood, the academy had moved to leased quarters in Burbank many years earlier. The offer of a brand-new facility for the academy and its Television Hall of Fame proved irresistible and the $500-million project was launched.

A 22-acre site on Lankershim Boulevard was acquired, and in honor of its theme tenant the project was named The Academy. The first phase was completed in 1990, closely supervised by Adkins, who had moved his own offices directly across the street in 1986 and who became The Academy's first tenant, followed closely by the Academy of Television Arts and Sciences, which occupies some 10,000 square feet of space.

In addition to its headquarters and the Television Hall of Fame, the Academy also has a 600-seat theater. Plans for expansion were also included, with the Academy having the options of taking additional space and/or buying the entire facility. Another major feature, certain to become an entertainment industry landmark and an attraction for photography buffs from all over the world, is a 26-foot-tall replica of the famous Emmy statue, symbol of television excellence.

Completion of the Kensley Group's Academy, as significant as it is, marks only the halfway point in what Adkins sees as a 20-year-long project. When completed at the turn of the century, the mixed-use development will include more than 2 million square feet of office space, almost 200,000 square feet of prime retail and restaurant space, a 200-room hotel, 400 residential units, and nearly 5,000 parking spaces.

Despite its magnitude, The Academy represents only one part of Adkins' commitment to North Holly-

A 26-foot-tall Emmy statue was unveiled on August 7, 1990, to adorn the new home of the Academy of Television Arts & Sciences on Lankershim Boulevard.

wood. A member of the board of directors of the North Hollywood Chamber of Commerce, he was one of the originators of its annual and highly successful Charity Star Scene event. He also helped launch the chamber's Major Business Association. In all his North Hollywood endeavors, he has indeed accomplished what he envisioned more than a decade ago, a goal "to make a significant impact on the community."

North Hollywood Carburetor and Ignition

North Hollywood Carburetor and Ignition has been a family-owned and operated company since its founding in 1937 by William A. Adams and his two sons, Vernon and Alvin, as a small battery, ignition, and carburetor repair center and wholesale parts jobber. The original location was at the corner of Lankershim and Chandler. When William died in 1940 his sons took over the operation, and in 1945 Vernon bought out his brother.

In 1947 Vernon and his wife, Louva, under whose direction the company had grown from three to 15 employees, moved the business to its present location at 5535 Lankershim Boulevard. Vernon was in charge of the shop, while Louva ran the office.

All service work is now performed at the new 6,000-square-foot facility.

In 1948 their son, Merlin, representing the third generation, joined the company, as did his wife, Vera, who assisted Louva in the office.

In the late 1960s Vernon and Louva retired, as a fourth generation began to get active in the business. During their high school and college days, all three of Merlin and Vera's children, two sons and a daughter, worked at the company. The sons later chose other careers but daughter Marsha stayed on, joined by her husband, Bob Miller, in 1974, after he completed a five-year tour in the U.S. Navy.

Bob Miller started in the service department, working his way up to his present position as president. Marsha is secretary, Merlin is chairman of the board, and Vera is vice president. The company has continued to grow and now has more than 30 employees.

By 1979 the company had completely outgrown its quarters and built a large, modern service facility across the street on Tujunga Boulevard. The original facility was converted to office space and the parts department, while all service work was moved to the new 6,000-square-foot, 13-stall facility, operating as North Hollywood Auto Repair. The company is a GM-authorized service center, certified by the Southern California Auto Club, and licensed as a state smog, brake, and light center.

The parts business, operating as North Hollywood Auto Parts, has also grown substantially. More than 19,000 part numbers, worth more than $600,000, are in stock. Many national original equipment lines, including AC, Delco, and Motorcraft are carried, and the fully computerized operation includes direct lines to the GM parts depot in Detroit. The company, which also stocks many import parts, sells primarily to garages, car dealers, service stations, and fleets.

Family members have long been involved in community activi-

Once the center of the company's operations, the original facility was converted in 1979 to office space and a parts department.

ties. Vernon Adams served many years ago as president of the North Hollywood Lions Club and his son, Merlin, is a past president of the North Hollywood Optimist Club and past district governor of Optimist International. Merlin is also a past president of the Optimists Boys Home in Highland Park and has been active in scouting for 45 years. In 1979 he was chosen by the Universal City/North Hollywood Chamber of Commerce as its Man of the Year.

Merlin has also served as president of the California Automotive Wholesalers Association. A retired colonel in the U.S. Air Force Reserve, he served six years on active duty during World War II and the Korean War.

His son-in-law, Bob Miller, is a past president of the North Hollywood Jaycees and the North Hollywood Kiwanis Club. He has also served on the board of directors of the Universal City/North Hollywood Chamber of Commerce.

For more than 50 years, the descendants of North Hollywood Carburetor and Ignition founder William Adams have served North Hollywood well. With Bob and Marsha Miller's two sons, representing the fifth generation, now working part time at the company while completing their education, that tradition appears likely to continue long into the future.

Texaco Inc.

Universal City was still ranch land and North Hollywood was a tiny community called Lankershim/Toluca when Texaco Inc. was formed in 1902. With initial capital of $3 million, the Texas Company was born, succeeding the Texas Fuel Co., formed a year earlier on the heels of the first major oil strike in Texas.

After a shaky start the company grew rapidly, and by 1905 had extended its operations to European markets. By the end of 1908 its sales operations in the United States covered all except five western states.

Around this time, an asphalt salesman in St. Louis first used the word "Texaco" as a product name after seeing it as a cable address. By 1906 the company had registered it as a trademark, and three years later was using what would become one of the nation's most famous and enduring symbols, the Texaco red star with a green "T." The name became so widely recognized that in 1959 the company was officially renamed Texaco Inc.

Texaco made its entry to California in 1928 when it acquired California Petroleum Corporation, extending its market area to all 48 states. The acquisition included producing wells, casing-head gasoline plants, pipelines, tankers, ocean terminals, and extensive marketing facilities throughout the western states. Texaco was the first and only oil company to sell its products directly in every state. In the 1930s it owned or leased more than 4,000 gasoline stations, which it began to call "service stations" to replace the term that had been in common use, "filling stations."

Today Texaco Inc., headquartered in White Plains, New York, is a worldwide, multibillion-dollar organization and one of the largest industrial corporations in the United States.

In 1985 Texaco selected 10

ABOVE: The first office of the Texas Company was opened in 1902 in Beaumont, Texas.

Universal City Plaza, a 36-story office tower, as the location for the Western Region headquarters of its subsidiary, Texaco Refining and Marketing Inc. The building was constructed in a joint venture with MCA, Inc.; Texaco became the first tenant. Today it employs about 500 people, including legal and tax personnel, at that location.

From 1958 until taking occupancy of the Universal City building in September 1985, regional headquarters had been at 3350 Wilshire Boulevard in Los Angeles. Prior to that time, Los Angeles operations had been located at Ninth Street and Broadway.

The arrival of Texaco in Universal City not only added a major employer to the area but a good neighbor as well. Texaco has had a long and distinguished history of community involvement, and Universal City/North Hollywood quickly became a beneficiary of that policy.

Students from area schools were among the first to benefit. Texaco is an active participant in the Regional Occupation Program of the Los Angeles Unified School District, in which high school students from North Hollywood come to Texaco for vocational training that supplements their education. The

RIGHT: Texaco's western headquarters building from 1928 to 1957 was at 929 South Broadway in Los Angeles.

success of that program is measured by the fact that more than a dozen of Texaco's permanent Universal City employees are graduates of the program.

Texaco also participates in the Adopt-A-School program, conducting monthly tours for students from Virgil Junior High School. The company also recognizes a student and teacher of the month and honors a student and teacher of the year. In addition, Texaco is spearheading a scholarship program for local students.

The company also allows free use of its conference rooms and other facilities by dozens of nonprofit groups, public agencies, and other organizations. Included among the regular users are the Los Angeles Police Department, Family Services of Los Angeles, and the California Highway Patrol.

Activities of this nature have brought the company many awards and commendations. In 1988 the Building Owners and Managers Association recognized Texaco's headquarters as a Building of The Year by

ABOVE: From 1958 to 1985 Texaco's western offices were located at 3350 Wilshire Boulevard in Los Angeles.

RIGHT: Texaco's current western region offices are at 10 Universal City Plaza in Universal City.

conferring its Pueblo Award for the building most involved with the community.

Texaco representatives also participate actively in charitable, cultural, civic, and business projects. The United Way receives substantial annual contributions both from the corporation and from its employees. Texaco also provides support for the arts, such as the Hollywood Bowl, the Los Angeles Music Center, and the Los Angeles Philharmonic Orchestra, following a long-standing tradition of its parent company.

For more than 50 years, Texaco Inc. has sponsored live New York Metropolitan Opera radio broadcasts, bringing opera into millions of American and Canadian homes every Saturday afternoon. Launched

in 1940, that sponsorship has continued without interruption, making it the longest association of any company with an artistic group in the history of broadcasting. In 1990 Texaco was honored for its involvement by OPERA America, a nonprofit organization comprised of 118 opera companies.

Western Region personnel have held leadership posts in a variety of local business groups, including the Universal City/North Hollywood Chamber of Commerce and the Valley Industry and Commerce Association. In 1989 Texaco was the lead

sponsor for the Charity Star Scene, the major fund-raising event for the charitable foundation established several years ago by the Universal City/North Hollywood Chamber of Commerce. Its generosity toward that cause earned Texaco an award as the chamber's Corporation of the Year for 1989.

Though a relative newcomer to Universal City/North Hollywood, Texaco Inc. has clearly demonstrated the good-neighbor policy that has been its hallmark across the United States for virtually all of the twentieth century.

Hewlett-Packard Company

It was a flip of the coin that determined whether Dave Packard's or Bill Hewlett's name would go first when the two men decided to go into business together. Classmates at Stanford University where they received their electrical engineering degrees in 1934, they formed the Hewlett-Packard partnership officially on January 1, 1939.

The new company, with $538 in working capital, was launched from a rented garage at 367 Addison Avenue in Palo Alto, California. The site is now a state registered historical landmark, recognized as the birthplace of "Silicon Valley."

The first Hewlett-Packard product was an audio oscillator providing higher performance than competing instruments in measuring the frequency of sound, and at a much lower price. A second version brought an order from Walt Disney Studios for eight oscillators, used in the hugely successful animated film, *Fantasia*, featuring stereophonic sound.

The new company was on its way. It quickly outgrew the garage, and after renting space for a time built the first of its own buildings, a 10,000-square-foot facility, where, by 1943, close to 100 people were working two daily shifts. In 1944, sales topped one million dollars for the first time.

Bill Hewlett and Dave Packard had barely closed that first Disney sale when they were introduced to a man who would have a major impact on their company. Back in 1933, while they were still students at Stanford, Norm Neely had founded Neely Enterprises as a manufacturer's representative for companies selling audio equipment to the newly emerging movie industry.

While on a sales trip to Northern California, Neely visited the Palo Alto garage and agreed to represent the fledgling company as its first sales rep. Working closely together, the two companies grew rapidly, and in 1962 Neely Enterprises was acquired by Hewlett-Packard and became the Neely Sales Region, encompassing the western United States. As a tribute to the major contributions of its founder, the Neely name was retained, unlike the other, geographically designated sales regions.

Today the Neely Sales Region, a one-billion-dollar-plus sales arm of the company, is headquartered at 5161 Lankershim Boulevard in North Hollywood. Its staff of nearly 3,600 people,

Norm Neely (left) founded Neely Enterprises in 1933 and later became the fledgling Hewlett-Packard Company's first sales representative. He and Bob Boniface (right), Neely's first region general manager, discuss plans for the organization's first headquarters site in North Hollywood in 1955.

Among those celebrating the 50th anniversary of Neely Enterprises in 1983 are founder Norm Neely (center), and Hewlett-Packard co-founders Bill Hewlett (far left) and Dave Packard (far right).

more than 300 in North Hollywood, operates from 42 sites in 14 states.

Neely Enterprises first came to North Hollywood from Hollywood in 1955. For 30 years it operated from a large Spanish-style building built by Norm Neely on Lankershim Boulevard and fondly called "Casa de Neely."

Norm Neely retired many years ago and now lives in San Diego. But the organization he built still continues to be guided by his principle that "the customer must be made to feel that we did a little bit better than he expected of us." One reason he blended so well with Dave Packard and Bill Hewlett is that he subscribed wholeheartedly to their style of management, a style that is known far and wide as "the HP way," that has contributed so much to the company's success.

Hewlett and Packard are still involved with the company they started more than a half-century ago that has become an international giant and one of California's largest businesses. Both are quick to credit "the HP way" for much of their success. "I feel that in general terms it is policies and actions that flow from the belief that men and women want to do a good job, a creative job, and that if they are provided the proper environment they will do so," says Hewlett. "But that's only part of it. Closely coupled with this is the HP tradition of treating each individual with consideration and respect, and recognizing individual achievements."

Sheraton Universal

Since it first opened its doors in February 1969, the Sheraton Universal Hotel has been one of the most successful in the worldwide chain operated by Sheraton Hotels. Jointly owned by MCA and ITT Sheraton, the hotel is the only one in the world located on a motion picture and television studio lot, that of Universal Studios.

It is an appropriate location, for the Sheraton Universal is synonymous with the entertainment world. Its grand opening celebration, billed

The 469-room Sheraton Universal Hotel is located on the lot of Universal Studios and is the official hotel of Universal Studios Hollywood. The 21-story tower affords views of the Hollywood Hills and the San Fernando Valley.

as "the most festive party in Hollywood history,"lasted three days and attracted hundreds of top stars in the world of the theater, motion pictures, and television, plus many dignitaries from around the world.

The 20-story tower sits on a Universal City hilltop overlooking the Hollywood Hills and much of the San Fernando Valley. Adjacent to the white concrete tower is a three-story poolside lanai wing. Built at a cost of $15 million, the hotel contains 446 guest rooms, including suites. Amenities include 24-hour room service,

Telly Savalas, popular for his role in television's "Kojak," is a resident of the Sheraton Universal Hotel. Telly's A Sporting Bar is named after him and displays sports memorabilia from sports teams in the Los Angeles area. Photo by Balfour/Godwin

a heated outdoor pool and spa, and exercise, sauna, and game rooms.

Less than five minutes away from the front door is the famous intersection of Hollywood Boulevard and Vine Street in Hollywood, with downtown Los Angeles only 11 miles away.

On grounds adjacent to and surrounding the Sheraton Universal, visitors are able to enjoy in the world-famous Universal Studios Tour. Conducted in open-air trams, the tours offer behind-the-scenes views of television and movie making, and the fortunate visitor will often come face-to-face with one or more of the industry's stars.

Many of those same stars are regular patrons of the hotel, some of them maintaining permanent suites in the tower so they can quickly get to the studio for early morning calls.

In 1990, after 21 years of out-

standing service and hospitality, the Sheraton Universal underwent what was described as "the most expensive facelift in Hollywood." The complete renovation cost $17 million, more than the entire cost of the original construction. All guest rooms, suites, and meeting rooms, as well as the lobby and restaurant, were completely refurbished. Upon completion of the enormous project, the hotel was proud to announce that "the glitz and glamour are back."

The former "Four Stages"restaurant became the home of "Telly's"Sports Bar, named in honor of Telly Savalas, a celebrity resident of the hotel for two decades. The former Cafe Universal is now the California's Restaurant, where guests may dine indoors or at poolside. The Roof Garden, one of the area's most popular locations for social events, was also redecorated.

In addition to its well-earned fame as "The Home of The Stars," the Sheraton Universal enjoys an outstanding reputation as a business hotel and regularly plays host to a variety of trade associations and other groups. Tourists who come from around the world to visit Universal Studios and such other nearby attractions as the Hollywood Bowl and Magic Mountain are also regular guests.

The Sheraton Universal has several meeting rooms, ranging in size from less than 500 square feet all the way up to the 10,300-square-foot Grand Ballroom, which can accommodate more than 1,000 guests. Over the years, the latter has been the site of many of the entertainment world's most glamorous events, for the Sheraton Universal is truly the "Hotel of the Stars."

Beverly Garland Hotel

What do a well-known movie and television actress, a singing cowboy turned broadcaster and baseball executive, and a legendary baseball player/manager have in common? All three of these celebrities, Beverly Garland, Gene Autry, and Casey Stengel are part of the history of the Howard Johnson Plaza Hotel, located at 4222 Vineland Avenue in North Hollywood, adjacent to the Hollywood Freeway.

Better known as the Beverly Garland Hotel, the project was developed and is owned by the actress and her husband, Fillmore P. Crank, Sr. They acquired the seven-acre site in 1967 from Gene Autry, who had purchased it years earlier from the Weddingtons, one of the pioneer families in North Hollywood. When Autry changed his plans to locate television station KTLA on the site, he sold it

to Crank and his wife.

Crank, a University of Southern California graduate, had been in the construction business since the end of World War II and was planning to build apartment houses on the newly acquired property. Its 900 feet of freeway exposure, however, made it less than an ideal site for residential development. That's when Casey Stengel entered the picture.

The Baseball Hall of Famer and former New York Yankee manager was on the board of directors of Glendale-based Valley National Bank, which financed the purchase of the land. Seeing the property, he suggested that the Cranks build a hotel.

When you come to Hollywood, a warm welcome awaits you in the quiet of a country garden.
4222 Vineland Avenue, North Hollywood, California

It proved to be excellent advice.

Once the necessary zoning variances were obtained, Howard Johnson officials were approached and quickly approved Garland and her husband as franchisees. Crank supervised the total construction, and Garland was responsible for interior decor, color coordination, and interior appointments. In February 1972 the beautiful new Beverly Garland Hotel opened its doors.

Looking back, Garland says, "Those were most exciting years, and suddenly there it was. Our complex of lovely buildings, beautifully landscaped, with a putting green, swimming and wading pools, two fine tournament tennis courts, and 262 rooms and executive suites in the 7-story high-rise building. Surrounding the building are sprawling, low-level out-buildings containing a

dining room, cocktail lounge, hotel offices, and the meeting rooms in our conference center. All the rooms have the cozy balcony/patios we had envisioned."

Garland and her husband, both native Californians, are actively involved in the management of their property. The actress, who also remains active in her chosen profession, was born in Santa Cruz and raised in Glendale, and began her career at age 18. In 1954 she was nominated for an Emmy for her performance in the initial episode of the TV series "Medic." It was a turning point in her career.

She has starred in nearly 50 motion pictures and hundreds of television programs. In 1957 she starred in her own TV series, "Decoy," and later appeared as a regular panelist on the charade show, "Stump The Stars." Probably her best known television role was as the wife of Fred MacMurray's character on the popular TV series, "My Three Sons," which ran until 1972. Also, Beverly starred with Kate Jackson in the TV series, "Scarecrow and Mrs. King."

During her career she has performed with many top stars in the entertainment world, including Bing Crosby, Frank Sinatra, Humphrey Bogart, and Fredric March. In January 1983 she was honored by having her star placed in the Hollywood Walk of Fame.

On May 23, 1960, she married Fillmore Crank, a Southern California native who started in the construction business after serving in the U.S. Air Force (then the Army Air Corps) during World War II. At the time of their marriage, he was a widower with two children, Cathleen and Fillmore Jr. The latter is now married to actress Tina Cole, who portrayed the stepdaughter on "My Three Sons," and is now Beverly's real-life stepdaughter-in-law. Garland and Crank also have two other chil-

dren: a daughter, Carrington, and a son, James. Carrington is now starring on the NBC hit, "Santa Barbara."

The success of the North Hollywood venture prompted Garland and Crank to build a second hotel. The Beverly Garland Motor Lodge, a 216-room complex of three three-story buildings and a conference center opened in Sacramento in 1981. An independent facility, it is managed by Fillmore Crank, Jr., who also supervised its construction. An Air Force veteran like his father, he also helped supervise the construction of the North Hollywood property.

The Beverly Garland Hotel has twice been expanded and is now conservatively valued at more than $30 million. Strategically located close to dozens of major Southern California attractions, it is an extremely popular spot for tour groups. Garland herself is a spokeswoman for the National Tour Association and travels all over the country speaking about the benefits of escorted tours and how to select the best ones.

Garland and Crank have also

The Beverly Garland Hotel, in the heart of the movie and television capitol of the world.

been strong supporters of their Universal City/North Hollywood community. For many years Garland has been the honorary mayor of North Hollywood and her husband has been named Man of The Year by the local YMCA. Many local organizations conduct meetings and other functions at the facilities, lured no doubt by the country-club atmosphere and excellent service. The hotel has also received a beautification award from the city of Los Angeles.

Being good hosts as well as good neighbors are top priority items for Beverly Garland and Fillmore Crank, as well as for other members of the family. "It's been a family affair right from the start," says Garland. "We're involved on a daily basis. We make sure our guests get what they want, friendly and professional service and attention. And I think guests can feel that the moment they check in."

Medical Center of North Hollywood

The Medical Center of North Hollywood (MCNH) is a 182-bed facility that has been serving San Fernando Valley residents since its founding in 1952. On September 1, 1980, the hospital was acquired by American Medical International (AMI), which owns and operates many health care facilities across the United States.

Since its acquisition by AMI, MCNH has undergone major remodeling, renovation, and expansion of all its facilities and is recognized for its high-quality service, patient care, and superior management. About 70 percent of the 600-member medical staff are board certified in a wide variety of specialties. They are assisted by an expanded nursing staff of 250, giving MCNH one of the highest nurse/patient ratios of any hospital in the San Fernando Valley.

The entire staff of 700 people is directed by an administrative team with a combined total of more than 50 years of medical management experience and advanced degrees in business, health care, and hospital administration.

A major focus of all hospital personnel is a unique "guest services" approach to patient care. MCNH has introduced such amenities as free limousine transportation for patients

The Medical Center of North Hollywood has been serving San Fernando Valley residents with its caring touch since 1952.

MCNH's recent redecorating and remodeling is representative of the hospital's commitment to the highest quality of patient care.

to the hospital for admission and back home after their stay. Outpatient surgery patients are offered a free overnight stay with meals, and for all patients current movies are available through the hospital's Video Theater.

Room service is also provided, including a newspaper, coffee, and juice delivered to the patients each morning and a chocolate truffle each evening. Gourmet chefs are also on staff, working with hospital dietitians to improve food taste and presentation, within necessary medical limitations.

The facility's excellent reputation for cost-effective, guest-oriented care has resulted in contracts with almost all major PPOs and HMOs. In addition, MCNH has been granted full three-year accreditation by the Joint Commission on Accreditation of Healthcare Organizations.

Among recent major renovations and expansion have been the new state-of-the-art Birthing Care Center, a Laser Institute, improved emergency room services and facilities, a Same Day Surgery and Gastrointestinal Center, a free health screening center—Testing 1 2 3—in the Sherman Oaks Fashion Square Mall, an Eating Disorders Center, and a Physician Referral Program.

MCNH also demonstrates a strong commitment to the community it serves, regularly opening its doors to provide meeting space for groups such as Alcoholics Anonymous, local chambers of commerce, seniors' groups, and business organizations. MCNH actively participates in the Universal City/North Hollywood Chamber of Commerce and has been a major contributor to its Charity Star Scene, an annual fundraising event for a variety of charitable purposes.

The hospital is also active in the Studio City Chamber of Commerce and is a major sponsor of its annual 10-K run, the proceeds of which are donated to Vital Options, a support group for young cancer patients.

The MCNH motto, "Growing to Meet Your Family's Needs," exemplifies the hospital's commitment to innovative medical care combined with a caring touch—a combination that has made Medical Center of North Hollywood AMI one of the premier health care facilities in the San Fernando Valley.

Patrons

The following individuals, companies, and organizations have made a valuable commitment to the quality of this publication. Windsor Publications and the Universal City—North Hollywood Chamber of Commerce gratefully acknowledge their participation in *Universal City and North Hollywood: A Centennial Portrait.*

Beverly Garland Hotel*
Brite Lite Neon Corporation*
Frazier Aviation*
Hewlett-Packard Company*
Hurley, Grassini & Wrinkle*
Kensley Group*
MCA Inc.*
Medical Center of North Hollywood*
Mooney & Murphy*
North Hollywood Carburetor and Ignition*
Sheraton Universal*
Texaco Inc.*

VDA Property Company*
Weddington Investment*

*Partners in Progress of *Universal City and North Hollywood: A Centennial Portrait.* The histories of these companies and organizations appear in Chapter 7, beginning on page 93.

ABOVE: Established in the 1890s, the Weddington store was the primary east Valley outlet for more than 30 years. Courtesy, Weddington Family Collection

BELOW: T.W. Herron's Meat Market & Grocery was a thriving North Hollywood business in 1915. Courtesy, Weddington Family Collection

Appendix

The Chamber of Commerce—1914-1990

For more than 80 years, beginning in 1910 when the organization was known as the Lankershim Businessmen's Association, the Chamber of Commerce has led the fight to make Universal City—North Hollywood a better place to live and do business. Past presidents have represented all walks of business: merchants, bankers, S&L executives, realtors, auto dealers, developers, lawyers, doctors, corporate executives, insurance executives, industrial businessmen, newspaper publishers, airlines executives, restaurateurs, distributors, stockbrokers, small business executives, and CPAs. There have been 52 presidents.

A Fourth of July celebration brought Secretary of Commerce William McAdoo to Lankershim School in 1924. Also present were the school's principal, Mr. Killion, and Jim Wilson, president of the local chamber of commerce. Courtesy, Weddington Family Collection

Lankershim Businessmen's Association, 1910-1914
C.C. Bowerman

Lankershim Chamber of Commerce, 1914-1927
1914-23	Jim Wilson
1924	C.C. Bowerman
1925-26	Forest Hicks
1927	Guy Weddington

North Hollywood Chamber of Commerce, 1927-1985
1927-29	Guy Weddington
1930-31	George Williamson
1932-33	Hall Rathbun
1934	Clarence Kennedy
1935-36	Martin Pollard
1937	William Freeman
1938	Ted Rathbun
1939	Ray Whitson
1940	William McCann
1941	E.F. Oldfield
1942	T.J. Laughlin
1943	C.L. Schofield
1944-45	R.J. Leckband
1946-47	R.N. Denaple

1948	Martin Pollard
1949-50	C.S. Newberry
1951-52	R.E. Gulbranson
1953	H.J. Penfield
1954	T.W. Clarke
1955	John Tuttle
1956	H. Geyer
1957	R.W. Denaple
1958	John Price
1959	B.S. Hand
1960	Everet Carpenter
1961	Everet McIntire
1962	Jack Elliott
1963-64	R.A. Quisenberry
1965-67	Eddie Holohan
1968	Al Dilernia
1969	Gerald Cutter
1970	Ed Weary
1971	Lloyd C. Bauman
1972	Gary Leary
1973	Roy Sorensen
1974	Clinton L. Johnson
1975	Lois Ortiz
1976	Jim Charter
1977-78	Joe Hurley
1979	Phyllis Roberts
1980	Guy Weddington McCreary
1981	Jack De Bar Smith
1982	Fred Massimini
1983	Bob McKarney
1984	Fred Sanborn
1985	Art Sweet

Universal City—North Hollywood Chamber of Commerce, 1985-Present
1985	Art Sweet
1986	Fred Bower
1987	Fred Sanborn
1988	Nancy Schmidt
1989	Harry Myers
1990	Bob Freman
1991	Tom Soule

First Woman on the Chamber's Board of Directors
1943   Jane Paxton

Women's Chamber Division, 1970-1982
1970   Phyllis Roberts

Retiring chamber of commerce president Roy Sorensen (second from left) turns over the gavel to president-elect Clinton L. Johnson during the 1973 chamber ceremonies. Actress and honorary mayor Beverly Garland (center), master of ceremonies Johnnie Grant, and chamber of commerce vice president Lois Ortiz look on. Courtesy, Universal City—North Hollywood Chamber of Commerce

1971	Madeline Thomas
1972	Freda Jones
1973	Cindy Campbell
1974	Peggy Ingraham
1975	Doris Schmidt
1976	Ruth Caprio
1977	Diane L. McCreary
1978	Kay Dohren
1979	Richie Brown
1980	Sheila Parker
1981	Jo Koebel
1982	Irmie Sofroniew

Honorary Mayors of North Hollywood

During Ted Rathbun's term as Chamber president in 1938, he selected the first Honorary Mayor, setting a precedent throughout the San Fernando Valley. What follows is the most complete record available:

1938-39	Glenda Farrell (actress)
1940-42	Gene Autry (actor)
1943-44	Gordon Jenkins (songwriter)
1951-52	Elyse Knox (actress) (Tom Harmon, husband)
1958-64	Verna Felton (comedienne, actress)
1965-66	Arthur Wong (actor, restaurateur)
1967-69	Yvonne De Carlo (actress)
1970	Elana Verdugo (actress)
1971	Dick Whitinghill (radio announcer)
1972	Andy Griffith (actor)
1973-91	Beverly Garland (actress, hotel owner)

Ambassadors of Goodwill
1965-66	Verna Felton
1967-90	Arthur Wong

Honorary Sheriff
1969-84	Nudie Cohn ("Country Western Tailor to the Stars")

Long-term Service Individuals
Margaret Barry, Assistant Manager
Ruth Ennis, Secretary
Barney Oldfield, Manager

Current Staff
Marjorie Roye Balas, Office Manager
Donald B. Eitner, Executive Vice President

North Hollywood Chamber of Commerce president Roy Sorensen proudly introduced the "Men of the Year" recipients Fred Massimini (left) and Bill Felts (right) at a 1973 banquet. Courtesy, Universal City—North Hollywood Chamber of Commerce

Bibliography

A Daughter of the Snows: The Story of the Great San Fernando Valley. N.P.: Security Trust and Savings Bank, 1923.

Andrés Pico papers. Huntington Library, San Marino, Calif.

Bancroft, Hubert Howe. *History of California.* Volumes 18 to 24, of 39 volumes. San Francisco: History Company, 1882-1891.

Bearchell, Charles A., and Larry D. Fried. *The San Fernando Valley: Then and Now.* Chatsworth, Calif.: Windsor Publications, 1988.

Bigelow, John. *The Life of John Charles Fremont.* New York: Derby and Jackson, 1856.

Bryant, Edwin. *What I Saw in California.* New York: D. Appleton and Company, 1848.

Caughey, John, and Norris Hundley. *California.* Fourth edition. Englewood CLiffs, New Jersey: Prentice-Hall, 1982.

Eyre, Alice. *The Famous Fremonts and Their America.* Boston: Christopher Publishing House, 1948.

Farnham, J.T. *Early Days of California.* Philadelphia: John E. Potter, 1859.

Guinn, James. *A History of California and an Extended History of Los Angeles and Environs.* Three volumes. Los Angeles: Historic Record Company, 1915.

Hill, Laurance. *La Reina.* Los Angeles: Title Insurance and Trust Company, 1931.

Hirschhorn, Clive. *The Universal Story.* New York: Crown Publishers, 1983.

James, George Wharton. *Fremont in California.* San Francisco: Fremont Hotel, 1903.

Jorgensen, Lawrence C., ed. *The San Fernando Valley: Past and Present.* Los Angeles: Pacific Rim Research, 1982.

Keffer, Frank. *History of the San Fernando Valley.* Glendale, Calif.: Stillman Printing Company, 1934.

Lankershim *Laconic.* Various editions.

Lankershim *Press.* Various editions.

Los Angeles Times. Various editions.

Mayers, Jackson. *The San Fernando Valley.* Walnut, Calif.: John D. McIntyre, 1976.

Nadeau, Remi. *Los Angeles: From Mission to Modern City.* New York: Longmans, 1960.

Nevin, David. *The Mexican War.* Alexandria, Virginia: Time-Life Books, 1978.

Nevins, Allan. *Fremont: The West's Greatest Adventurer.* New York: Harper and Brothers, 1928.

North Hollywood *Press.* Various editions.

Pitt, Leonard. *Decline of the Californios.* Berkeley and Los Angeles: University of California, 1968.

Richards, Irmagarde. *Early California.* Sacramento: California State Department of Education, 1950.

Robinson, John W. *Los Angeles in Civil War Days: 1860-65.* Los Angeles: Dawson's Book Shop, 1977.

Robinson, W.W. *Ranchos Become Cities.* Pasadena, Calif.: San Pasqual Press, 1939.

Rolle, Andrew F. *California.* Third edition. Arlington Heights, Illinois: AHM Publishing Corporation, 1978.

————. *Los Angeles: From Pueblo to City of the Future.* San Francisco: Boyd and Fraser, 1981.

The Valley of San Fernando. The San Fernando Valley Chapter of the Daughters of the American Revolution, 1924.

Valley Times. Various editions.

Index